D0197938

# READING IN COMMUNION

# READING IN COMMUNION

## Scripture and Ethics in Christian Life

Stephen E. Fowl
and
L. Gregory Jones

WILLIAM B. EERDMANS PUBLISHING COMPANY
GRAND RAPIDS, MICHIGAN

Copyright © 1991 by Stephen E. Fowl and L. Gregory Jones

First published in Great Britain 1991 by SPCK, London,
as part of the series *Biblical Foundations in Theology*,
edited by James D. G. Dunn and James P. Mackey.
SPCK
Holy Trinity Church
Marylebone Road
London NW1 4DU

This edition published in the U.S.A. 1991
through special arrangement with SPCK by
Wm. B. Eerdmans Publishing Co.
255 Jefferson Ave. S.E.
Grand Rapids, Michigan 49503

All rights reserved.
No part of this book may be reproduced, stored in a retrieval
system, or transmitted — in any form or by any means, electronic,
mechanical, photocopying, recording, or otherwise — without
permission in writing from the publisher.

Printed in the United States of America.

ISBN 0-8028-0597-3

*For Jim Buckley*

# CONTENTS

# Editors' Foreword

The aim of this series is to bridge the gap between biblical scholarship and the larger enterprise of Christian theology. Whatever the theory or theology of the canon itself, Christian theologians have always seen in the Bible their ultimate court of appeal, and exegetes have rightly expected their work to contribute directly to a better theology for each succeeding century.

And yet the gap remains. Theologians from the beginning, the greatest as well as the least, have been guilty of forcing their preferred conclusions upon a biblical text which they could have better understood. And the more professional biblical scholars, too anxious perhaps for immediate theological impact, have often been tempted to produce Old or New Testament theologies which in the event owed too little to the rich variety of their authoritative texts, and too much to prevailing theological fashions. Co-operation between a critical scholar of the texts and a critical commentator on theological fashions was seldom evident, and few individuals have ever been able to combine both of these roles successfully.

*Biblical Foundations in Theology* attempts to address this problem by inviting authors from the disciplines of Biblical Studies or Systematic Theology to collaborate with a scholar from the other discipline, or to have their material reviewed in the course of composition, so that the resultant volumes may take sufficient account of the methods and insights of both areas of enquiry. In this way it is hoped that the series will come to be recognized as a distinctive and constructive contribution to current concerns about how, in the modern world, Christianity is to be lived as well as understood.

JAMES D. G. DUNN

JAMES P. MACKEY

# Introduction

Christians have often been described as 'people of the Book'. This is typically a claim about the centrality of Scripture for Christian life. While we do not disagree that Scripture is central to Christian life, we want to go further. The vocation of Christians is to *embody* Scripture in the various contexts in which they find themselves.

Discerning *how* to go about embodying Scripture, however, is a complex matter. In part, the complexities are the result of differences between the contexts in which the Bible was originally written and read and the variety of contemporary contexts in which Christians read Scripture. This is a point that contemporary professional biblical scholarship has made with considerable power. It is one of the reasons why simplistic, fundamentalist attempts simply to replicate the demands of Scripture in the present fail adequately to articulate the relationship between Scripture and Christian life.

Nevertheless, the complexities involved in embodying Scripture were recognized long before the rise of critical scholarship around the time of the Enlightenment. This is because, while there certainly is a temporal distance between the settings of Scripture and our own, the most important complexities are not historical but moral and theological.

Rather than allow the temporal distance between the biblical texts and contemporary contexts to paralyze us, we argue in this book that Christians need to develop the moral and theological judgement which enables faithful discernment of Scripture's claims on contemporary life. We contend that the development of such judgement requires the formation and transformation of the character appropriate to disciples of Jesus. This requires the acquisition of a very different set of skills, habits and dispositions from those required of the professional biblical scholar. Further, Christians develop such character in and through the friendships and practices of Christian communities. Hence the importance of 'reading in communion'.

We make this case in six interrelated chapters. In Chapters 1 and 2 we provide methodological reflections on the relationship between Scripture and ethics. We situate our position in relation to contemporary conceptions of Christian ethics and of biblical interpretation. It is here that we first emphasize the role of Christian communities for learning how to read Scripture wisely so that Christians might live faithfully before God.

Chapter 3 takes this point further in two ways. On the one hand, we describe moral discontinuities raised by the failure of Christians to embody faithful living before God. On the other hand, we suggest how and why Christians need to recover the centrality of Christian communities if they are to embody faithful interpretation of Scripture for Christian life and ethics.

The recovery of Christian communities, however, is not sufficient. We can still expect large-scale disagreements within and among Christian communities about how best to understand and perform Scripture. In Chapter 4 we describe some interpretive disputes within Scripture and in contemporary life. We argue that issues of interpretation and issues of character are intimately related in such disputes. We point out the dangers of interpretive self-deception, arguing that communities which are closed in on themselves may require the presence of prophets whose voices they are unwilling to hear.

Thus in Chapter 5 we argue that Christian communities need to cultivate an openness to outsiders. This requires that Christians learn how to listen to, and if need be translate, the voices of outsiders. These voices can challenge and correct their interpretive practices, reminding them of the provisionality of their readings and performances of Scripture.

Finally, in Chapter 6 we provide an account of Dietrich Bonhoeffer's life and his death at the hands of the Nazis. We argue that Bonhoeffer was an exemplary performer of Scripture. His life and death exemplify the importance of reading in communion.

We realize that our emphasis on reading in communion will not in itself solve particular disputes that arise among Christians in specific contexts. We do think, however, that our arguments provide a way forward in understanding the relationship between Scripture and ethics in Christian life.

We have taken seriously the editors' invitation to write a book *together*. Rather than providing alternating perspectives, we have struggled to create a single text – no small task for an Anglican and a United Methodist. Further, we have attempted to write a text that is accessible and suitable to professionals and lay people alike. We hope that this text can be read and studied both in seminars for graduate students and in church study-groups.

Insofar as we have achieved this, we could not have done so without the help of numerous people. We are indebted to the following people for comments on, and criticisms of, earlier drafts of the manuscript: James P. Mackey and James D. G. Dunn, the series editors; A.K.M. Adam, Clift Black, Charles Bobertz, Mark Brett, Jim Buckley, Michael Cartwright, David Cunningham, Jean Bethke Elshtain, Louise Foster, Stanley Hauerwas, Richard Hays, Phil Kenneson, Mary Jane Kreidler, Charles Marsh, Richard Vance, Gerald West, and Jonathan Wilson. We would like to hold each of these people accountable for any failings this book might have, but we can't. Suffice it to say that any failings are the responsibility of the other author.

We are grateful for our colleagues here at Loyola. Their presence provides a lively and stimulating environment in which to work. We are particularly grateful to David Roswell, Dean of the College of Arts and Sciences, for his support, particularly the research grants which allowed us to devote undivided attention to writing the book.

We also want to thank the people at SPCK and Wm. B. Eerdmans for their patience with, and encouragement of, this project.

This book is dedicated to our chairperson, Jim Buckley. He is a remarkable friend whose persistent good humour, sharp intellect, and wise guidance have improved this book in innumerable ways. He handles the often onerous duties of chairing our department with extraordinary grace. He takes his vocation as theologian with the utmost seriousness without taking himself too seriously. He is a theologian both for the Church and for the academy.

# 1

## Living Faithfully Before God:
## Scripture and Ethics in the Context
## of Christian Life

Some twenty-five years ago James Gustafson lamented the gap between biblical studies and Christian ethics. He observed that:

> In spite of the great interest in ethics in the past thirty years, and in spite of the extensive growth of biblical studies, there is a paucity of material that relates the two areas of study in a scholarly way. Writers in ethics necessarily make their forays into the Bible without the technical exegetical and historical acumen and skills to be secure in the way they use biblical materials. But few biblical scholars have provided studies from which writers in ethics can draw.[1]

Whatever else can be said about the relation between biblical studies and Christian ethics, however, it no longer suffers from inattention. In the years since Gustafson made his remark, both biblical scholars and Christian ethicists have made significant attempts to remedy the situation. Indeed, there has been such attention to the issue that William Spohn recently published a book devoted to the question *What Are They Saying about Scripture and Ethics?*[2]

While there is much to be learned from these attempts, there are some significant problems with the methods and presumptions upon which much current work on the use of Scripture in Christian ethics rests. In fact, casting the issue in terms of 'use' (as in the *use* of Scripture in Christian ethics) suggests that Scripture is something out there waiting to be 'used'. All that is needed is the proper method which will (1) excavate the meaning of the Bible, (2) apply that meaning to this or that situation, and (3) identify how the meaning found in the Bible ought to be understood in relation to other possible sources of guidance.

We think this approach is problematic. Thus in this chapter

we point out the inadequacies of the ways in which ethics and interpretation have been typically understood in modern scholarship. We will also show why a significant part of the 'gap' that is presumed to exist between contemporary ethics and biblical interpretation results more from our conceptions of ethics and interpretation than from problems inherent in either area.

## THE QUEST FOR AN ETHICAL METHOD

The dominant modern conceptions of the scope of ethics have been predicated on the view that ethics is concerned with right actions and decisions and with developing the appropriate method for arriving at their rightness. Moreover, the focus has been on decisions that individuals must make regardless of their particular social and historical contexts. These conceptions were largely presumed in discussions of the place of Scripture in Christian ethics which arose in the middle of this century.[3] We cannot pretend to provide either an adequate analysis of modern conceptions of ethics or an account of how and why they came to be dominant in modernity.[4] Nevertheless, we need to identify how the modern emphasis on decisions made by isolated individuals has distorted our understanding of the place of Scripture in Christian ethics.[5]

Articles in the mid-1960s by Edward LeRoy Long Jr and James M. Gustafson provide typologies of the place of the Bible in Christian ethics. In spite of their variations, these typologies share the common presumption that the Bible's role is located in relation to particular decisions made by isolated individuals.

Take, for example, Gustafson's widely influential contrast between seeing the Bible as a 'revealed morality' or as a 'revealed reality'. If Scripture is the revelation of a 'morality', Gustafson contends, then decisions are made according to the moral laws, precepts and commands given in Scripture. On the other hand, if Scripture is the revelation of 'reality' (understood as theological principles used to interpret what 'God is doing'), then decisions are made not by finding binding moral laws and commands in the Bible but by discerning the theological context that illumines the contemporary issues.[6] Typically this is done by determining how what God 'did' through (what Gustafson calls) the 'great variety' of moral values, norms, and principles in the Bible is related to what God 'is doing' in the contemporary situation. The Bible does not, in this view, provide the primary standard for decision-making or even the content of the decision. Rather, it provides a background horizon that informs or illumines a decision-making process the resolution of which will be adjudicated on other grounds.[7]

It is perhaps not surprising, given these options, that scholars have tended to reject accounts that see the Bible as prescribing moral rules, principles and commands. Instead, they favour accounts oriented towards basic notions and values that can inform contemporary decision-making. Indeed, Spohn concludes his survey of arguments about the place of Scripture in Christian ethics by noting:

> Contemporary Christian ethics does not use the Bible as a sourcebook of moral norms. Most of the authors we investigated propose an illuminative rather than a prescriptive use of Scripture. Decisions should be made in light of the central concerns and commitments of the canonical text, but decisions are not directly derived from biblical prescriptions.[8]

This approach characterizes all those specific proposals that argue for an illuminative use of Scripture. Even those texts which attempt to present a putatively neutral typology of the ways the Bible relates to Christian ethics tend to be structured so that the reader will be more inclined to reject a prescriptive account in favour of an orientation towards basic notions and values.

Regardless of whether one sees the Bible's relation to Christian ethics as illuminative or prescriptive, the view of ethics which these options presume focus on the decisions that an individual must make. Even more, the underlying presumption of the whole enterprise has been that these methods ought to be employed by individuals regardless of their particular social and historical contexts.[9] This presumption that the isolated, autonomous individual is the primary focus has guided the discussion about the place of the Bible in Christian ethics in at least three ways.

First, ethicists have sought a method that any individual can employ in making decisions. If the right method is adopted, then the individual's particular character and social situation are of only secondary relevance to the decision-making process. They should not decisively affect either the description or the evaluation of the situation being addressed.

Second, when ethicists have turned to the Bible, they have often presumed that it is addressed primarily to independent individuals. This has tended to be the case regardless of whether the particular material being assessed is the Ten Commandments, the teachings and life of Jesus, or one of Paul's letters. The ethically valid and important passages have to do, it is argued, with the situation of the individual in relation to God and/or in relation to another individual.[10] Jewish or Christian communities are relatively insignificant, if they have a place at all.

Third, the focus on the individual entails that a person's ethical decision-making can and ought to be subjected to scrutiny through the use of critical reason formalized in clear and precise methods. That is, a person's decision-making should be defensible in terms that all people could accept. The Bible may be one resource for discovering the principles and/or values a person ought to follow, but it cannot be determinative. The standards for ethical decision-making, so it is argued, should transcend the particularistic appeals of Jewish or Christian communities. Thus, ironically, on this conception discussions of the Bible's role in Christian ethics belong equally well, and perhaps even better, in contexts such as the modern academy which purport to be 'free' of any particular commitments.

Clearly there are occasions when the individual is the primary locus of ethical decision-making and/or the primary interpreter of the Bible.[11] But it is a mistake simply to presume the centrality of the individual. Such a presumption fails to account for the ways in which we learn or fail to learn to make wise moral judgements in and through the particular circumstances in which we find ourselves. More specifically, this presumption that the individual is central does not account for the ways people have read the Bible in and through particular communities, particularly ecclesial ones, in the past.[12]

Most importantly, we contend that a strong focus on the individual distorts Christian readings of Scripture. For example, consider the numerous tortured accounts of the role of the Sermon on the Mount in relation to individual Christians. Scholars have characterized the Sermon's demands as hyperbolic ideals, counsels of perfection, or claims whose real purpose is to point out the inevitability of our moral failure. But all of these accounts neglect the fact that Matthew 5—7 is addressed to a community of believers and only a community can faithfully embody its demands. This does not dissolve the Sermon's interpretive problems, nor does it guarantee that we will faithfully embody the Sermon's demands. Nevertheless, the community does provide the necessary standpoint for making the Sermon intelligible and practicable in the present.[13]

That is, Scripture is primarily addressed not to individuals but to specific communities called into being by God. This is so not only in relation to particular texts like the Sermon on the Mount but to Scripture more generally.[14] It is in these respects we contend that a strong focus on the individual presents a distorted conception of ethics and of Scripture's relation to Christian ethics.

Further, while Christian ethics involves the making of decisions, the desire for general rules and formulae for making decisions neglects the controversial status of moral descriptions. This is important because the very articulation of the decisions people face depends on how one describes the contexts, convictions, and commitments involved in any particular situation.

Take the decision of whether or not to commit suicide. As Alasdair MacIntyre has shown, cultural and temporal differences suggest that the very shape of this decision will vary. MacIntyre contrasts the self-inflicted death of Minamoto no Yoshitsune in twelfth century Japan with the death of an anonymous Japanese person of today.[15] Yoshitsune's death was performed to preserve his honour in the face of imminent defeat and done in accordance with Buddhist scriptures, whereas MacIntyre's modern Japanese person takes his own life because he is unable to cope with the burdens of trying to succeed. MacIntyre draws the conclusion that the two deaths, and hence the evaluation of the two decisions, are quite different. Yoshitsune's death is a reflection of triumph over imminent defeat while the modern Japanese person's is a reflection of total defeat. Moreover, the former is an act that can express the achievement of a supreme good, while the latter expresses the frustration of an individual's practical reasoning by external social circumstances. Because Yoshitsune's action is contextualized within the habits, dispositions and convictions of a Buddhist nobleman in medieval Japan, the decision facing him is very different from that facing the anonymous Japanese person of today who is largely divorced from those contexts and convictions.

Though MacIntyre clearly shows the ways in which particular social settings and ways of construing the world affect the kinds of decisions we face, we want to go further and suggest that the description 'suicide' is not equally applicable to both cases. Because Yoshitsune's taking of his own life was bound up with his conception of honour, it is better described as *hara kiri* than as suicide. Thus Yoshitsune would not have described his action as a justifiable exception to some generally recognized moral rule against suicide, but as the positive expression of a commitment to which he was morally bound by honour. Yoshitsune's decision was whether to act honourably or dishonourably, not whether or not to commit suicide.

Hence, because there is no way to talk about moral decisions apart from people's contexts, convictions, and commitments, a preoccupation with decisions made by isolated individuals distorts our conception of ethics in general and the relation of Scripture to Christian ethics in particular. An adequate conception of ethics requires attention to issues of character and the formation of character in and through socially-embodied traditions.

We are not alone in these judgements. Over the past several years, many people have recovered the notion, going back at least to Plato and Aristotle, that ethics needs to attend not simply to the quandaries and decisions a person faces but also to the character of the person who faces those quandaries and decisions.[16] Moreover, scholars have started to recognize the central role communities play in the formation of character and in ethical deliberation.

Thus two of the more recent and most sophisticated proposals for the place of the Bible in Christian ethics, Thomas Ogletree's *The Use of the Bible in Christian Ethics* and Bruce Birch's and Larry Rasmussen's *Bible and Ethics in the Christian Life*, attend both to the formation of character and the importance of community.[17] Although there is much to be learned from each of their different perspectives, a preoccupation with decisions made by individuals continues to shape both books. Consequently, despite their recognition of the importance of character, both fail adequately to explicate the relationship between character and community in Christian ethics.[18]

This is because in different but overlapping ways Birch/ Rasmussen and Ogletree contend that attention to character needs to be put alongside such other elements as rules, principles, values and assessments of consequences. Thus both accounts propose a pluralistic ethical method that they claim is more comprehensive in articulating the various themes of an individual's moral life than is an exclusive focus on *either* decision-making (through a focus on principles or consequences) *or* the formation of character.

But such proposals for a 'comprehensive pluralism' in ethics are deeply problematic.[19] The notion of a comprehensive pluralism misleadingly suggests that there are two (or more) separate spheres of ethics, one having to do with the formation of character, another having to do with rules and principles, another having to do with the assessment of consequences. A comprehensive pluralism fails to recognize that character should not be so much a component in an ethical method as a different perspective on the shape of ethics itself.[20] It is not something that can be combined with a rule-based or consequence-based ethical method without loss. Rather, character is formed in and through socially-embodied traditions. Such traditions provide particular conceptions of the Good toward which we are striving, through which we form our character, and against which we assess the correctness of particular judgements.

This is not to say that moral rules are unimportant in an account of ethics. Contrary to a comprehensive pluralism's presumption, however, the importance of moral rules is not *independent* of the formation of character in socially-embodied traditions. Moral rules embody the wisdom of a tradition over time. They are thus contextualized within the friendships and practices of particular communities. The obligations specified by those rules are the obligations required by the exercise of the virtues of character. Moral rules are in principle open to revision because new situations and the particular discriminations made by people of practical wisdom may lead either to reformulations of the rule or to the formulation of new rules.[21]

Though they are open to revision, a tradition's moral rules are also often both relatively stable and authoritative.[22] Their authority comes not only from the judgements of people of practical wisdom, but also (and more determinatively) from their place in a tradition's moral vision. And such moral rules are partially constitutive of the tradition's identity. Thus, as MacIntyre has argued, some moral rules have enduring validity:

> An enduring moral principle or rule is one which remains rationally undefeated through time, surviving a wide range of challenges and objections, perhaps undergoing limited reformulations or changes in how it is understood, but retaining its basic identity through the history of its applications. In so surviving and enduring it meets the highest rational standard that can be imposed, and there clearly comes a time in the history of a morality when the possibility of some particular principle or rule being either overthrown or radically emended, although still open in principle – quite new forms of challenge can never be finally ruled out – provides no ground at all for any limitation upon our practical allegiance to that principle or rule.[23]

Within any socially-embodied tradition the relations between rules and particular judgements is complex, and in any given case either may take priority.

Does that mean that there are, after all, some moral rules that all people *must* accept? There is no *a priori* way to answer such a question. Because there are overlaps among moral traditions (and hence also overlaps among accounts of character and the virtues), it should not surprise us to discover that there may well be agreement about at least some moral rules across some traditions. Such agreement cannot be presupposed, because the moral rules need to be properly specified so that there is a relatively determinate range of applications of the rule. But we only discover such agreements through conversation and argument with adherents of those socially-embodied traditions.

Our view does not imply a relativism about morality. Indeed we think that Christian claims about the moral life are universal in the sense that all people are called to live as disciples of Jesus Christ. We reject the notion of universality only insofar as someone claims that there are rules, principles, claims, values and the like that are detached from particular traditions and/or that all people *must* accept simply by virtue of being human. Even the process of specifying the universal implications of moral rules is inextricably tied to the descriptions that particular traditions offer.

An additional problem with proposals for a comprehensive pluralism is that they fail to recognize that moral descriptions are socially embedded. They continue to presume that situations, decisions and moral rules are somehow 'out there' in a morally neutral way. This is particularly evident in the arguments of Birch/Rasmussen's book. They note that Scripture can actually 'create' moral problems, and they recognize that various kinds of social structures decisively influence character. However, though both claims would seem to point to the particular and controversial status of moral descriptions, such awareness does not really affect their conception of ethics or of the role of Scripture in Christian ethics.

This is evident in the abstract way they describe community. Community is 'a synonym for social relatedness', and Christian community is that 'community-creating human relatedness which is a consequence of the impact of Jesus'.[24] Such a view does not take adequate account of the differences between the 'social relatedness' we have simply as members of the human species and the particular relations we are to have with fellow followers of the crucified and risen Christ. Taking community as a 'synonym for social relatedness' precludes Birch and Rasmussen from accounting for the ways people learn to describe actions, situations and lives in terms which other people would contest.[25]

By contrast, we argue that the activity of moral description requires the formation of character within the particular communities that embody a tradition's moral vision. Indeed, there will inevitably be conflicts about moral descriptions even among diverse and competing communities within a tradition. However, the range of such conflicts is likely to be more restricted. Moral descriptions will be controversial regardless of whether the descriptions concern the process of characterizing a situation in one way rather than another, delineating what is to count as a virtue and what a vice, or giving form both to actions and to lives.

For example, Christians have an important stake in insisting that marriage is a covenant, not a contract. The description of marriage as a contract comes from modern liberal societies, and such a description erodes the sense of commitment and fidelity that has long characterized Christian uses of the term 'marriage'. It is significant that many of the problems associated with 'marriages' in contemporary American society arise from presumptions that the relationship is a contractual agreement entered into by separate individuals. In this context we have seen the development of that virtual guarantee of a future divorce – the 'pre-nuptial' agreement. By contrast, Christians have a stake in preserving the description of marriage as a covenant and the virtues of character that are the ingredients in such a description (e.g., fidelity, courage, hope, love).[26]

Instead of a comprehensive pluralism in ethics, we contend that there is no way of understanding issues (or interpreting texts, as we shall argue below) apart from particular social contexts and particular ways of construing the world. People do not come to decisions or to texts in a vacuum or as isolated individuals; they come as people with particular histories and commitments and specific habits, dispositions and convictions. The ways people describe and evaluate issues, texts, and even their lives are significantly shaped by material circumstances and by the kinds of people they are and want to become. Obedience to rules and assessments of consequences will invariably play a role in such descriptions and evaluations. But they do so in the context of people exercising the virtues of character as those have been shaped and nurtured by particular communities that are the social embodiments of a tradition's moral vision.

For these reasons, we contend that the search for a context-independent ethical method is bound to fail. There is no way to provide a neutral, objective, or even phenomenological method that encompasses the kinds of social, historical, ideological and theological contexts in which people live. These contexts not only affect how people understand their own lives and the issues they face, they also affect the ways people write and read texts. Further, there may be sharp contrasts between the social settings in which a text was produced and the contexts in which it is read. What people are looking for in a text, or what they are able to see and understand, is affected by their material circumstances, by the kind of people they are, and by the kind of people they want to become.

We have outlined some of the problems that have plagued contemporary conceptions of Christian ethics, particularly as those problems bear on discussions of Scripture. We think there are similar problems which plague contemporary conceptions of biblical interpretation. In the following chapters we will develop a more complete account of the centrality of Christian communities for understanding Scripture in Christian ethics. But first we need to explain some of the problems of contemporary biblical interpretation, particularly as those problems bear on discussions of Christian ethics.

## THE QUEST FOR AN INTERPRETIVE METHOD

In the last 250 years debates about the meaning of a text have tended to dominate biblical interpretation. Such debates are related to a curious inversion which has taken place in the history of biblical interpretation. Initially, interpreters operating within relatively limited ecclesial contexts produced numerous different readings. Over time, the numbers of different social locations in which people interpreted the Bible have increased while the number of interpretive options pursued in each location have decreased.

The diversity of locations in which the Bible is now interpreted ranges from the professional 'Q Seminar' of the Society of Biblical Literature to various televangelists. While diverse in numerous respects, interpreters in both these contexts, surprisingly, agree on their interpretive aim. They are all trying to uncover what they call 'the meaning' of the text under consideration. The common presumption uniting the professional exegete and the televangelist (despite their differing interpretive results) is that the text is a relatively stable entity which has a single 'meaning'.

The ecclesial contexts in which the Bible was initially interpreted provided both a location in which interpretation could be applied and communal standards against which interpretation could be judged. In the light of the numerous locations in which the Bible is now interpreted, such controls are not widely available. As a result, both professional and confessional interpreters have diligently sought 'the meaning' of the Bible which could act as a control on interpretation.[27]

Academic biblical scholars in particular have engaged in a persistent quest for a method which an isolated autonomous individual can use to uncover 'the meaning' of a text regardless of whether any specific use will be made of that text.[28] Anyone familiar with biblical studies, however, will recognize that in spite of two centuries of increasing sophistication we still have large and intractable disagreements about meaning in general and about the meaning of any biblical text in particular.

This situation is not the result of a failure of method which we could expect to be corrected given enough time. The problem with the quest for a method for determining the meaning of a text is that we cannot agree on what the meaning of a text would be. Until we know what it is we are looking for, we cannot develop a method for finding it. Our disagreements are not really about method; they are about notions of the meaning of a text. From Friedrich Schleiermacher and Benjamin Jowett in the nineteenth century to Krister Stendahl and E. D. Hirsch in the present day, we are now heirs to dozens of theories about what the meaning of a text is and how it should be found.[29] Further, with a little healthy scepticism it is possible to show that all of these general theories about the meaning of a text are to some degree arbitrary and question-begging.

Rather than pursue this illusory quest for the meaning of a text, we recommend that we think in terms of 'interpretive interests'.[30] One can pursue any number of interpretive interests; we can rationally evaluate the results of such pursuits; and we need never call these results 'the meaning of the text'. People can pursue a wide range of interpretive interests, but there is no way to ascribe the term 'meaning' to one of these interests at the expense of the others without begging the question of what the meaning of a text is.

Our aim is not to undermine the unproblematic and conventional ways we use the term 'meaning' in everyday conversation. Rather, our point is that when we have interpretive disputes, generalized 'theories of meaning' should not be used to rule other interpretive options out of court.

As an example of what we are arguing for, imagine convening a conference of a physicist, a Marxist, a psychoanalyst, a Christian advocate of 'creation science' and an Augustinian Christian. The aim of the conference would be to discuss the opening chapters of the book of Genesis. We would not be surprised to find widespread disagreements among these interpreters about the best reading of Genesis. Even so, nothing will be gained by an interpreter simply asserting that their reading is *the* meaning of the text. The interpreters will only clarify and perhaps resolve their differences to the extent they can articulate more precisely what their interpretive aims are when they read the Bible. In the course of their discussions they may even find that some of them (e.g., the physicist and the Augustinian Christian) are pursuing different yet not incompatible interests.

Once we acknowledge the plurality of interpretive interests, we need not treat alternative interpretations as failed attempts to discover the meaning of a text. One of the residual benefits of this is to rehabilitate the history of the exegesis of Scripture. While we need not always agree with the readings of such interpreters as Origen, Aquinas, Teresa of Avila, or Luther, discerning and critically reflecting on their interpretive interests can help to clarify and enrich our own readings.[31]

Even so, recognition of the plurality of interpretive interests does not resolve the important question, 'What interpretive interest should one pursue in any given situation?' Is it simply a matter of subjectively and relativistically choosing on the basis of some kind of consumer preference? After all, while any particular way of reading a specific text can be rationally judged to be good or bad, adequate or inadequate, according to the aims it seeks to achieve, we seem to lack any way of arguing that one way of reading a text is better than another.

If we are to say anything concrete about the role of Scripture in Christian ethics, we will need to articulate why people might adopt one interpretive interest rather than another. Given what we have said so far, however, it is clear that a generalized theory or method of interpretation is not going to provide an answer. Rather, our claim is that an answer will only be found within the political constitution of the various contexts in which interpretation takes place.[32]

In fact, the very shape of the question concerning which interpretive strategy to adopt in any situation will be determined by the political nature of the context in which interpretation takes place. Further, the resources available to any particular group of interpreters to answer this question will depend on the nature of the arrangements they form and sustain in the act of interpreting. Thus there is no interpretive practice which is free of some kind of political presumptions. Hermeneutics is inevitably, though not restrictively, a 'political' discipline.

The basis for these contentions about the political nature of interpretation is the recognition that interpretation, like all true science, is a social activity. As such, it is subject to the political arrangements in which people interpret. This claim does not ignore the fact that people read texts on their own, in the privacy of their own home, for their own edification and enjoyment. But such readings must be subjected to scrutiny, examined, debated, and discussed by other people to have the character of interpretation.[33]

As a social activity, interpretation is confirmed, constrained, and determined by the political constitution of those contexts in which interpretation takes place. Further, as we noted above, when we move from this point to answering the question of which interpretive interest to adopt in any specific situation, the political nature of any particular context will both shape the sort of question this becomes and constrain the types of resources available to any group of interpreters.

For example, the political arrangements and ideologies of modern universities and professional societies have had a significant impact on the shaping of presumptions about biblical interpretation. Many 'professional' interpreters of the Bible are in universities that are either publicly funded or have only loose ties to particular ecclesial bodies. Such scholars are typically members of professional societies such as the Society of Biblical Literature, the Society of New Testament Studies, the Society of Old Testament Studies, and so forth. In principle, such a context is designed to allow individual scholars to pursue whatever interpretive interest captures their fancy. Many scholars consider this freedom the primary gain in releasing biblical scholarship from the control of the Church.[34]

Within such a political arrangement, any particular interpretive task can be carried out more or less adequately. The relevant parties can rationally argue that one way of carrying out that task is better than another. Within this arrangement, however, the only ostensible reason for adopting one interpretive interest over another is that it is interesting to sufficient numbers of scholars to sustain its practice. The only reasons a university or a professional society could rationally give for discouraging someone from pursuing a coherently formulated interest would be practical ones (e.g. not enough time, money, space, etc.).[35]

A liberal institution such as a university or a professional society has a very limited stock of arguments to draw on in refusing to recognize and support a particular interpretive interest if it is not to transgress its own principles of pluralism and act arbitrarily.[36] More particularly, however, the demands of particular institutions constrain the kind of interpretation that is done. For example, to keep one's position in a college or university it is typically assumed that one will read papers at conferences and publish articles and books. But publishing the results of one's interpretive practice is significantly dependent on the relevance of that practice to the interests of the editors of the journal and/or the chair of the committee that determines whose papers will be read. As we have already suggested, these constraints have meant that in modern Western societies discussions of biblical interpretation in general, and discussions of the place of the Bible in Christian ethics in particular, have been carried on primarily within the presumptions and ideologies of liberal thought and practice.

But people have not often noticed the ways in which even criticism of some liberal ideas and practices of interpretation reflect other liberal presumptions and commitments. For example, Elizabeth Schüssler Fiorenza in her 1988 presidential address to the Society of Biblical Literature forcefully argued not only that biblical scholars have neglected their responsibilities to society, but also that the interpretive interests that have characterized critical scholarship for the last century have actually worked to obscure and minimize the social role of biblical scholarship. As these interpretive interests are being revised and replaced with the arrival on the critical scene of new interpretive interests, Schüssler Fiorenza urged her colleagues in the guild of professional biblical scholarship to order their interpretive interests in the light of their social responsibility.

> In short, if the Society were to engage in disciplined reflection on the public dimensions and ethical implications of our scholarly work, it would constitute a responsible scholarly citizenship that could be a significant participant in the global discourse seeking justice and well-being for all.[37]

Schüssler Fiorenza's criticisms are meant to undermine the view that any interpretation is valid simply if it is interesting. Even so, by appealing in a methodologically neutral way to notions such as 'the global discourse' that is seeking 'justice' and 'well-being' for all, Schüssler Fiorenza's rhetoric continues to reflect the desire for openness and pluralism that undergirds the political arrangements of the Society of Biblical Literature.

In this light, it is not hard to see that issues of biblical interpretation in general, and their relation to Christian ethics in particular, are cast differently in the context of particular Christian communities than in the context of the modern academy. While both institutions can be found within the same contexts of modern liberal societies, Christian communities are called to have political arrangements that are different from liberal societies and the ethos typical of modern universities.[38] Thus while both universities and Christian communities may in fact be beset by the same kinds of problems presented by the marketplace, bureaucracy and individual consumerism, Christian communities are called to have a politics that alters the settings in which interpretation of Scripture *should* take place.

That is to say, the question of which interpretive interest to adopt in any specific situation is quite different when asked about a Christian community's interpretation of its Scriptures than of a university department's or professional society's interpretation of the Bible. This is primarily because Christian communities already stand in a particular relationship to the Bible. For the university department or the professional society, the Bible is simply one of the texts on which scholars might exercise their interpretive interests. But the Bible constitutes the authoritative Scripture of Christian communities, and this makes a decisive difference. The life of Christian communities is to be formed and regulated by the interpretation of Scripture, though how that occurs and what kind of authority Scripture is taken to have is a controversial matter. What this suggests is that there is already an intimate relationship between the political constitution of Christian communities as a context of interpretation and the texts to be interpreted.[39]

In our view, the biblical texts, as Scripture, provide a canon for the Church. The canon provides the normative standard for the faith, practice and worship of Christian communities.[40] The notion of canon, however, is not simply a reference to a fixed list of books. A body of authoritative formulations takes on the character of canon when those formulations play a certain role for a particular group of people, not simply by existing as a list.[41] Thus as the Scripture of the Church, the Bible shapes the political contexts in which Christian communities should interpret.

Scripture not only shapes the political contexts of faithful interpretation, it also tells us who God is and how we ought to live in relation to that God.[42] Christian communities interpret Scripture, then, so that believers might live faithfully before God in the light of Jesus Christ. The aim of faithful living before the Triune God becomes the standard to which all interpretive interests must measure up.[43] One cannot begin to judge whether this standard is being achieved unless and until the interpretation of Scripture becomes socially embodied in communities of people committed to ordering their worship, their doctrines, and their lives in a manner consistent with faithful interpretation. Even then, what constitutes 'faithful living' is often a matter of dispute. Such disputes cannot be resolved either in the abstract or through *a priori* formulae. In Chapter 4, however, we offer reflections on particular disputes and where points of resolution might lie.

Unless Christian communities are committed to embodying their Scriptural interpretation, the Bible loses its character as Scripture. Without this commitment, Christian communities will lack the capacity to adjudicate interpretive disputes faithfully. No single interpretive interest can guarantee the maintenance of a community of faithful people. Unlike a university department or a professional society, the Church's interpretive practices are confirmed in the presence of communities of people committed to the Bible as their Scripture and actively engaging in the process of ordering their lives in accordance with those texts in the various situations in which they find themselves.

The aim of Scriptural interpretation is to shape our common life in the situations in which we find ourselves according to the characters, convictions, and practices related in Scripture. Because no one interpretive strategy can deliver *the* meaning of a text, there is no hard and fast method that will ensure faithful interpretation. No particular community of believers can be sure of what a faithful interpretation of Scripture will entail in any specific situation until it actually engages in the hard process of conversation, argument, discussion, prayer and practice.

Thus, we contend that the search for a context-independent interpretive method is bound to fail. There is no way to provide a neutral, objective or even phenomenological method that encompasses the kinds of social, historical, ideological and theological contexts in which people read and write texts. The ways in which people read and write texts are decisively shaped by material circumstances and by the kinds of people they are and hope to become. Interpretation, like ethics, requires attention to particular conceptions of communities in which people learn to read and write texts and learn to become this or that sort of person. We are convinced that such attention will provide the most adequate way to characterize the issues surrounding the place of Scripture in Christian ethics.

## CONCLUSION

Throughout this chapter we have argued that the search for a context-independent method for either ethics or interpretation is doomed to failure. We have further contended that there is no neutral or apolitical way of discussing ethics or doing interpretation, and that one of the problems of discussion about the Bible in Christian ethics has been that it has not paid sufficient attention to the politics of Christian communities.

But our arguments against the search for context-independent methods do not mean that we are against the importance of methodological reflection. Nor do we want to support anarchy or subjectivism in either ethics or interpretation. Rather, by seeing the task of interpreting Scripture in the contexts of Christian communities that are striving to live faithfully before God, we want to refocus the issues. In this light, the questions now focus upon how we enable wise readings of Scripture so that people can live faithfully before God. We have suggested that such questions cannot be separated from conceptions of the particular practices and contours of Christian communities. So it is that we now turn to an exposition of how we learn and/or fail to learn to become wise readers of Scripture in and through the friendships and practices of Christian communities.

## NOTES

1. James M. Gustafson, 'Christian Ethics', in *Religion*, ed. Paul Ramsey (Englewood Cliffs, NJ: Prentice-Hall, 1965), p. 337. A longer version of this essay can be found as 'The Changing Use of the Bible in Christian Ethics', in *Readings in Moral Theology No. 4: The Use of Scripture in Moral Theology*, eds Charles E. Curran and Richard A. McCormick SJ (New York: Paulist Press, 1984), pp. 133–50.

2. See William C. Spohn SJ, *What Are They Saying about Scripture and Ethics?* (New York: Paulist Press, 1984).

3. Explicit methodological reflection on the relations between Scripture and ethics began in the 1960s. The pivotal essays were by Edward LeRoy Long Jr, 'The Use of the Bible in Christian Ethics: A Look at Basic Options', *Interpretation* 19 (1965), pp. 149–62; James M. Gustafson, 'Christian Ethics' (see note 1), and 'The Place of Scripture in Christian Ethics: A Methodological Study', *Interpretation* 24 (1970), pp. 430–55; and C. Freeman Sleeper, 'Ethics as a Context for Biblical Interpretation', *Interpretation* 22 (1968), pp. 443–60. Gustafson's two articles have been reprinted (though the article 'Christian Ethics' is developed in a different form) in *Readings in Moral Theology No. 4*, eds Curran and McCormick, pp. 133–77.

4. For powerful accounts that differ in their descriptions and evaluations of ethics in modernity, see, for example, Alasdair MacIntyre, *After Virtue*, 2nd ed (London: Duckworth; Notre Dame, IN: University of Notre Dame Press, 1984); Jeffrey Stout, *The Flight From Authority: Religion, Morality and the Quest for Autonomy* (Notre Dame, IN: University of Notre Dame Press, 1981); Charles Taylor, *Sources of the Self* (Oxford: Oxford University Press; Cambridge, MA: Harvard University Press, 1989).

5. A helpful survey of the early discussions of the Bible and Christian ethics is found in chapter 2 of Michael G. Cartwright's Ph.D. dissertation, 'Practices, Politics, and Performance: Toward a Communal Hermeneutic for Christian Ethics' (Duke University, 1988), pp. 69–146.

6. One version of this view, which Gustafson does not discuss in any detail, can be found in many modern Roman Catholic accounts of natural law. In this view, the Bible deals mainly with humanity's supernatural end, whereas the natural law deals with moral issues and questions. In so far as the Bible is relevant to morality, it provides principles such as the Ten Commandments which can be discovered equally well through the use of 'untutored' reason and whose authority are in no way dependent on the Bible. We should note that such a view reflects 'modern' natural law theories, and not so much claims of natural law more generally. Modern natural law has tended to rely on a minimalist account, which presumes that reason does not need to be tutored. Such a view is more

dependent on the Enlightenment than someone like Aquinas. Hence modern natural-law accounts have tended to have a 'decisionist' bias similar to non-natural-law accounts. For an excellent analysis of modern natural-law theories and criticism of their heritage in the Enlightenment, see Russell Hittinger, *A Critique of the New Natural Law Theory* (Notre Dame, IN: University of Notre Dame Press, 1987); and 'Varieties of Minimalist Natural Law Theory', *The American Journal of Jurisprudence* 34 (1989), pp. 133–70.

7. See Gustafson's discussion of these issues in relation to the United States's invasion of Cambodia in 'The Place of Scripture in Christian Ethics: A Methodological Study'.

8. Spohn, *What Are They Saying about Scripture and Ethics?*, p. 134.

9. This point has been made by Michael G. Cartwright in a very suggestive way through the application of Fredric Jameson's criticisms of Northrop Frye's readings of the Bible to discussions about the place of the Bible in Christian ethics. See Cartwright, 'The Practice and Performance of Scripture', in *The Annual of the Society of Christian Ethics 1988*, ed D. M. Yeager (Washington, DC: Georgetown University Press), pp. 31–4.

10. For example, Gilbert Meilaender, who has been at the forefront in the movement to return the virtues and character to a central place in ethics and has written insightfully about such issues, still understands character and the shape of ethics in ways focused on the individual. In 'The Singularity of Christian Ethics', Meilaender notes the importance of moral formation, but then describes character in terms of the individual subject. Thus in his reading of Galatians 3 and 4, Meilaender fails to recognize that the texts' concern is with the Church as the reconstituted people of God, *not* (as he suggests) with two ways of picturing the individual believer's encounter with God. See 'The Singularity of Christian Ethics', *Journal of Religious Ethics* 17 (1989), pp. 95–120, esp. pp. 113–15.

11. For a strong defence of the importance of the individual, see Richard Mouw, *The God Who Commands* (Notre Dame, IN: University of Notre Dame Press, 1990). Even here, however, Mouw acknowledges that the most important commands in the Hebrew Scriptures are addressed primarily to a community (see p. 43). No one should dispute that Scripture addresses individuals, but that address is typically focused on forming and sustaining a faithful common life.

12. See Cartwright, 'Practices, Politics, and Performance', for excellent discussions of both Eastern Orthodox and Anabaptist understandings of the Bible.

13. For an example of an insightful reading of the Sermon in the context of Christian community, see Richard Lischer, 'The Sermon on the Mount as Radical Pastoral Care', *Interpretation* 41 (1987), pp. 157–69. See also Stanley Hauerwas, 'The Sermon on the Mount, Just War and the Quest for Peace' *Concilium* 215 (1988), pp. 36–43.

14. For example, Richard Hays has instructively and insightfully shown how Paul's readings of Scripture (our Old Testament) reflect not so much a christocentric reading (as has often been supposed) but an ecclesiocentric reading. As Hays shows, Paul sees both continuities and discontinuities between the people of Israel and the Church of Jesus Christ, but his overall perspective is shaped by an understanding that the Church is the reconstituted people of Israel. Paul's readings are carried out in the context of pastoral situations, and they are done in the service of forming communities of faithful disciples. See Hays, *Echoes of Scripture in the Letters of Paul* (New Haven, CT: Yale University Press, 1989).

15. See Alasdair MacIntyre, 'Positivism, Sociology, and Practical Reasoning: Notes on Durkheim's *Suicide*', in *Human Nature and Natural Knowledge*, eds A. Donagan, A. N. Perovich Jr, and M. V. Wedin (Dordrecht: D. Reidel, 1986), pp. 96–7.

16. See, for notable examples, Edmund Pincoffs, 'Quandary Ethics', *Mind* 80 (1971), pp. 552–71; Stanley Hauerwas, *Character and the Christian Life* (San Antonio, TX: Trinity University Press, 1975); Gilbert Meilaender, *The Theory and Practice of Virtue* (Notre Dame, IN: University of Notre Dame Press, 1984); and Alasdair MacIntyre, *After Virtue*.

17. Thomas W. Ogletree, *The Use of the Bible in Christian Ethics* (Oxford: Basil Blackwell; Philadelphia, PA: Fortress, 1983); Bruce C. Birch and Larry L. Rasmussen, *Bible and Ethics in the Christian Life*, revised and expanded edition (Minneapolis, MN: Augsburg Fortress, 1989). It may appear odd to cite Birch and Rasmussen as a recent proposal since the first edition of their book, published in 1976, was one of the earliest book-length studies of the Bible and Christian ethics. Even so, the 1989 edition represents such substantial changes that it is almost a new book rather than a new edition of an old book. And, it is significant to note, one of the primary changes in the book is a more central role for issues of character and community.

18. See the original edition of Birch/Rasmussen, *Bible and Ethics in the Christian Life* (Minneapolis, MN: Augsburg, 1976), p. 54, as well as the later edition, *passim*. See also Ogletree, *The Use of the Bible in Christian Ethics*, pp. 28–34.

19. Neither Birch/Rasmussen nor Ogletree use the term 'comprehensive pluralism' to describe their own approaches, though Ogletree does characterize his perspective as a working out of Edward L. Long Jr's proposal for 'comprehensive complementarity' in ethical theory (see Ogletree, *The Use of the Bible in Christian Ethics*, p. 45, n. 31). Characterizing their views as a desire for a 'comprehensive pluralism' suggests that they want both to incorporate all of these various factors *and* that, while these factors may be interrelated, each factor's importance is independent of the others.

20. Even John Howard Yoder, whose perspective has informed ours in

many ways, still seems to operate with a conception of character where it is merely one component alongside attention to rules and consequences. See 'The Hermeneutics of Peoplehood', in *The Priestly Kingdom: Social Ethics as Gospel* (Notre Dame, IN: University of Notre Dame Press, 1984), pp. 35–7. Yoder's own account of a hermeneutics of community operates with a much richer conception of character than his explicit discussion would seem to suggest.

21.  It should be noted that Ogletree recognizes the revisability of rules and the importance of practical wisdom. This leads us to wonder why he characterizes his discussion in terms of deontology and gives it such a prominent place in his argument. See Ogletree, *The Use of the Bible in Christian Ethics*, pp. 24–8 and also pp. 192–205.

22.  By contrast, an attempt to provide a tradition-independent account of moral rules and principles operates with the assumption that there are (at least some) moral rules and principles which are the ultimate authorities against which the correctness of particular judgements should be assessed. So, for example, Birch/Rasmussen argue that there are some principles such as truth-telling and promise-keeping which are 'simple requirements of daily existence itself' (rev.ed., pp. 55–6). Similar claims are also made by Meilaender, 'The Singularity of Christian Ethics', pp. 101–2, and by Paul Nelson, *Narrative and Morality* (University Park, PA: Penn State University Press, 1987), pp. 38ff.

But such a claim almost certainly does *not* mean that those principles are binding in all specific instances. Rather these principles are made systematically *in*determinate so that people from different and incompatible standpoints can accept them. As Alasdair MacIntyre has suggested, an independently-derived principle really functions as a claim that, for example, 'One ought to tell the truth, but there are a range of occasions on which truth-telling is problematic and then....' or 'One ought to obey the law, but there are a range of situations in which lawabidingness is problematic and then....' We could expect people to agree to abide by a principle whose range of application is indeterminate. Such indeterminacy, however, prevents the rule or principle from being specified so that its authority can be genuinely binding on moral judgement. See Alasdair MacIntyre, 'Does Applied Ethics Rest on a Mistake?' *The Monist* 67 (1984), p. 510.

23.  MacIntyre, 'Does Applied Ethics Rest on a Mistake?', pp. 508–9.

24.  Birch and Rasmussen, *Bible and Ethics in the Christian Life*, revised and expanded edition, pp. 17, 67.

25.  Alternatively, Ogletree's actual readings of Scripture suggest a greater sense of the centrality of Christian community in providing particular moral descriptions. Here Ogletree's significant and important insights about the controversial status of communities and descriptions are at odds with his pluralistic ethical method centered on the individual. See also Cartwright's criticisms of Ogletree, 'The Practice and Performance of Scripture', pp. 41–4.

26    READING IN COMMUNION

26. Consistent with the last paragraph, we would note that there are
    also differences within the Christian tradition about how best to
    characterize marriage (e.g. whether it is a sacrament). Even so,
    the range of conflicts over these descriptions is much narrower
    than between the Christian tradition taken as a whole and liberal
    societies.
27. For more detailed accounts of the effects of the Enlightenment and
    Romanticism on Biblical interpretation than we can give here see,
    for examples: Mark G. Brett, *Biblical Criticism in Crisis? The Impact
    of the Canonical Approach on Old Testament Studies* (Cambridge:
    Cambridge University Press, forthcoming); Hans Frei, *The Eclipse
    of Biblical Narrative* (New Haven, CT: Yale University Press, 1974);
    David C. Steinmetz, 'The Superiority of Pre-Critical Exegesis', *Ex
    Auditu* 1 (1985), pp. 74–82.
28. See also Chapter 1 of Charles M. Wood, *The Formation of Christian
    Understanding* (Philadelphia, PA: Westminster, 1981), for a similar
    argument with which we are in broad agreement.
29. Schleiermacher's lectures on hermeneutics were published pos-
    thumously and have recently been translated into English. See
    *Hermeneutics: The Handwritten Manuscripts*, ed. Heinz Kimmerle,
    tr. James Duke and Jack Forstman (Missoula, MT: Scholars
    Press, 1977). Jowett's essay, 'On the Interpretation of Scripture',
    appeared in *Essays and Reviews*, 7th ed. (London: Longmans,
    Green, Longman and Roberts, 1861), pp. 330–433. Stendahl's
    famous distinction between what a text meant and what it means was
    first presented in his article on 'Biblical Theology, Contemporary'
    in *The Interpreter's Dictionary of the Bible* vol. 1 (Nashville, TN:
    Abingdon, 1962), pp. 418–32. We include the literary critic E.
    D. Hirsch in this list of biblical scholars/theologians because his
    distinction between meaning and significance has been influential
    in debates about the meaning of the Bible. See Hirsch, *Validity
    in Interpretation* (New Haven, CT: Yale University Press, 1967),
    and 'Meaning and Significance Reinterpreted', *Critical Inquiry* 11
    (1984), pp. 202–25.
30. We take the phrase, and many of the ideas in this section, from
    Jeffrey Stout's 'What is the Meaning of a Text?', *New Literary
    History* 14 (1982), pp. 1–11. See also Mark Brett, 'Four or Five
    Things to Do with Texts: A Taxonomy of Interpretive Interests',
    and Stephen Fowl, 'The Ethics of Interpretation, or What's Left
    Over After the Elimination of Meaning', both in *The Bible in
    Three Dimensions*, eds D. J. A. Clines, S. E. Fowl and S. E.
    Porter (Sheffield: JSOT Press, 1990), pp. 357–77, and 379–98,
    respectively.
31. Once we do this, we will not be surprised to find that previous
    interpreters did not limit themselves simply to one reading of a
    text. Yet one could hardly characterize the history of Scriptural
    interpretation down to the Enlightenment as a period of interpretive
    anarchy.

32. The term 'political' here is used not with reference to contemporary partisan politics, but to designate the types of arrangements in which people live and in which they enact certain practices.

33. This is not a novel claim, nor is it limited to textual interpretation. Karl Popper has made a similar point in regard to the natural sciences. Popper asks us to imagine a Robinson Crusoe figure stranded on a desert island. Our Crusoe, who is both brilliant and well equipped, spends his time engaging in various sorts of experiments, rigorously recording his results. While we might be tempted to call this Crusoe a scientist, Popper notes that these experiments and results do not take on the character of science until they can be subjected to the critical appraisal of other scientists. Popper's point is not simply a point about the natural sciences. Rather it is an example of the general point about the social character of all knowledge. See Popper, 'The Sociology of Knowledge', in *The Sociology of Knowledge: A Reader*, eds J. E. Curtis and J. W. Petras (London: Duckworth, 1970), pp. 649–67.

34. Even a professional society like the Catholic Biblical Association now prides itself on being pluralistic. See Pheme Perkins' comments on this in 'The Theological Implications of New Testament Pluralism', *Catholic Biblical Quarterly* 50 (1988), pp. 5–23, esp. pp. 5, 14. This perception of gaining freedom from the control of the Church, however, may not bear the weight of historical scrutiny. See, for example, John Rogerson, *Old Testament Criticism in the Nineteenth Century: England and Germany* (London: SPCK, 1984).

35. Of course in addition to these, there exist a whole host of ideological factors that affect the political context of interpretation in modern universities, factors that we cannot attend to here but that none the less have had an important impact on shaping conceptions of interpretation and ethics.

36. We would, however, raise questions about the very notions of 'openness' and 'pluralism'. For example, see Cornel West's 'The Politics of American Neo-Pragmatism', in *Post-Analytic Philosophy*, eds John Rajchman and Cornel West (New York: Columbia University Press, 1985), pp. 259–75. A more direct attack on pluralism in literary studies is provided in Ellen Rooney's *Seductive Reasoning* (Ithaca, NY: Cornell University Press, 1989).

37. Elizabeth Schüssler Fiorenza, 'The Ethics of Interpretation: Decentering Biblical Scholarship', *Journal of Biblical Literature* 107 (1988), p. 115.

38. This does not presume that particular Christian communities only exist in relation to modern liberal societies. Indeed we think that Christians in the First World can and should learn a great deal about the relationship of Scripture to Christian ethics from listening to people in Christian communities which exist outside the spheres of liberal thought and practices.

39. Though as we will suggest in Chapter 3, the existence of Christian communities in modern societies is such that this 'political constitution' will need to be significantly rehabilitated if we are to enable

wise reading and performance of Scripture.

40. See James D. G. Dunn and James P. Mackey, *New Testament Theology in Dialogue* (London: SPCK; Philadelphia, PA: Westminster, 1987), p. 2, who use the term 'canon' in a similar way.

41. See Wayne Meeks's comment: 'A book or a formal list of documents is not a canon, unless there is a community that makes it authoritative' in 'A Hermeneutics of Social Embodiment', *Harvard Theological Review* 79 (1986), p. 182. It is surprising that within a few paragraphs of this definition of canon Meeks goes on to talk about a 'pre-canonical' phase in the life of the earliest Christians. While it is true that the earliest Christians did not have the list of books that constitutes the Christian canon today, they did have a body of authoritative formulations to which they struggled to order their faith and practice. These formulations functioned as the canon for the first believers and later developed into the formal list of books we know as the Christian canon today. We discuss issues of canon in greater detail in Chapter 2.

42. It is worth noting that this seems to have been one of the primary motivations in the establishment of the canonical texts that we now have. As George Lindbeck has argued, 'The rule of faith, in its various versions, articulated the liturgically embedded christological and trinitarian reading of the Hebrew scriptures; and the selection of certain writings out of the many then circulating which claimed apostolic status depended on their usefulness within the context of the *sensus fidelium* formed by this implicit or explicit rule of faith. (The use and therefore meaning of the text, be it noted, was the one it had in the canon-forming situation, not in some putative historically reconstructed one.)' 'Scripture, Consensus, and Community', *This World* 23 (1988), p. 7.

43. See, for example, Rowan Greer's summary of Augustine's argument in *On Christian Doctrine*: 'It will be seen that the signs of Scripture function properly when they rightly direct our attention to the Trinity, which can alone be enjoyed' in James L. Kugel and Rowan A. Greer, *Early Biblical Interpretation* (Philadelphia, PA: Westminster, 1986), p. 198.

# 2

## Reading in the Communion of Disciples: Learning to Become Wise Readers of Scripture

For Christians, interpreting Scripture is a difficult task. But it is difficult *not* because one has to be a specialist in the archaeology of the ancient Near East, an expert in linguistics, or a scholar of the literature of the Greco-Roman world. Though we will argue in this chapter that Christians can learn important things about the Bible from the investigations pursued by people who do have such expertise, they are not necessary for wise readings of Scripture. Rather, the interpretation of Scripture (which as we have suggested is different from interpreting the Bible) is a difficult task because it is, and involves, a lifelong process of learning to become a wise reader of Scripture capable of embodying that reading in life.

Learning to embody Scripture in our lives, both corporately and personally, requires that we develop specific patterns of acting, feeling and thinking well. This is an exercise in practical reasoning and depends on being able to judge a certain situation as being similar in some respect to another situation, moral maxim, or canonical text. The presence of such insight, however, presupposes a prior and ongoing formation and transformation in moral judgement.[1]

Some of the contexts of that formation and transformation occur in and through specific friendships and practices of Christian communities, as we will show in Chapter 3. At this point, however, it is important to indicate the link between Scripture and Christian ethics as it relates to the *necessity* of such formation and transformation.

## PRACTICAL WISDOM AND INTERPRETATION

There are several reasons why the interpretation of Scripture is an open-ended and controversial activity requiring the virtue of practical wisdom.[2] The first reason is that interpretation in general is always open-ended. We are never completely sure that we have interpreted someone's thoughts, feelings or actions (including our own) accurately. Thus as we have already indicated, there is always a need to check our interpretations over-against those of others, including our own earlier interpretations.

Second, the interpretation of Scripture is open-ended because Christian Scripture itself is a diverse, multi-stranded witness reflecting diverse social and historical circumstances. The scope of Scripture includes, for example, pre-exilic Israel and first-century Rome. Even Paul's letters address a wide variety of circumstances. Thus, as we shall argue in more detail later in this chapter, discerning the larger sense of Scripture and developing strategies for reading difficult texts in the light of that larger sense are complex and ongoing tasks.

Third, the persistence of temporal and cultural change ensures that the interpretation of Scripture will remain indeterminate. Simply to remain faithful our readings will need to change. Nicholas Lash makes this point in a lighthearted way in regard to ecclesiastical dress:

> If, in thirteenth-century Italy, you wandered around in a coarse brown gown, with a cord round your middle, your 'social location' was clear: your dress said that you were one of the poor. If, in twentieth-century Cambridge, you wander around in a coarse brown gown, with a cord round your middle, your social location is curious: your dress now says, not that you are one of the poor, but that you are some kind of oddity in the business of 'religion'. Your dress now declares, not your solidarity with the poor, but your amiable eccentricity.[3]

Lash's point is not an attack on the Franciscans, but a logical argument about how temporal and cultural change necessitates ongoing interpretation. The manner of dress needed to identify with the poor in contemporary Britain or America would be markedly different than it was in thirteenth-century Italy. Hence two different types of dress would be needed to continue identifying with the poor. As Lash incisively suggests, 'Fidelity to tradition, in action and speech, is a risky business because it entails active engagement in a process of continual change.'[4]

But fourth, and most decisively, the interpretation of Scripture is indeterminate and requires the moral formation and trans-formation of people's lives because of the manifold ways in which people do not judge wisely. More precisely, our complicity in sin leaves us captive to destructive patterns of life. Such captivity undermines our ability to read Scripture well. Liberation from our captivity requires an ongoing process of being formed and transformed by God's grace in and through the friendships and practices of Christian communities.

It is true that becoming a Christian involves living in a 'new' world. Indeed some have gone so far as to suggest that Scripture 'creates' a world,[5] or that Scripture 'creates' a community as the bearer of that world.[6] But that is in itself an insufficient characterization. Scripture does not 'create' anything *de novo*; in the encounter with Scripture, believers' 'old' selves and perceptions of reality are confronted with that new world. Hence the emphasis must be placed on *learning* to live in that world, for it involves not only discerning the 'new' world but also diagnosing what is wrong and corrupting about the 'old' one. Such learning is a lifelong process requiring as a necessary correlative, at least in most social settings, a rather extensive unlearning of believers' old habits, dispositions, and judgements. Thus the interpretation of Scripture is an ongoing task because appropriate discernment is a task that must be achieved in communities guided by the Spirit; it cannot be assumed, nor is it simply 'created'.

Both character and interpretive skill are formed in relation to each other over time, particularly as we engage in the process of learning to read Scripture wisely and unlearning the ways in which our lives have been corrupted.[7] This cultivation of practical wisdom sometimes requires us to separate ourselves from day-to-day activities and concerns.

We see an important example of this need in one of the Servant Songs of Isaiah (see Isa. 49.1ff.). The Servant is appointed to a task before birth (49.1, 5). Yahweh entrusts the Servant with a message to proclaim, making the Servant's tongue a sharp sword and making the Servant a polished arrow (49.2a, c). Such formation, however, takes place in secret, out of the way: 'in the shadow of his hand he hid me;...in his quiver he hid me away'

(49.2b, d). The Servant's mission is to recall and restore the people of Yahweh and, ultimately, to be a light unto the nations (49.6). In spite of the apparent failure of this mission, the Servant proves his character by recalling Yahweh's formative work in his life. The Servant ultimately rests in the knowledge that Yahweh is the one who has formed him for his mission and who ultimately ensures the success of that mission (49.5).

The formation that takes place in the Servant's life is carried out in hidden places: the womb, the shadow of God's hand, and as a polished arrow hidden in God's quiver. Such imagery is significant, for it suggests both the ways in which God forms and transforms our character for particular vocations and the importance of discovering 'hidden places' in which such formation and transformation can occur. These 'hidden places' can include such possibilities as the Wesleyan class meetings of early Methodism, patterns of regular retreats, and disciplined prayer. Even such acts as working in a soup kitchen can provide a 'hidden space' where Christians begin to discern more clearly what God is calling us to be and do.

There are at least two reasons why, as Christians, we should establish separate spaces where we can instruct and form each other to be disciples and wise readers. The first reason is pragmatic. That is, the formation needed to develop the character of disciples requires commitment and concentration that can best be achieved apart from the routines of everyday life.

The second reason is conceptual and is related to the fact that Christians are not called to manifest just any sort of character. Their lives are to be a faithful reflection of God's character. Ironically, the need for the type of separate space we are talking about is particularly urgent in those places where most people claim to believe in God. This is because of the heightened danger of that belief becoming acculturated and/or trivialized. When Christians are the only ones around who proclaim allegiance to the God of Jesus Christ, there is little chance of their knowledge of God becoming profaned through exposure to a non-Christian culture. The earliest Christians found themselves in this type of situation.

But if and when Christians find themselves in a context in which people both claim to know the God of Jesus Christ *and* attempt to reduce knowledge of God to a series of platitudes ranging from the inane to the incoherent, they must struggle to create a separate space in which they can teach each other about God away from the reductionistic practices and profaning tendencies which otherwise dominate their lives.[8] We think that the Church in Britain and the United States finds itself in this latter situation. But, as we will suggest in Chapter 3, we are also convinced that too few churches have recognized the need for a separate space devoted to forming people's character to be disciples of the Triune God.

When the early Christians found themselves in situations in which their talk about God was becoming less distinct from what their neighbors said about their god/s, they developed patterns of worship and life that would provide hidden spaces for the formation of disciples. Such a 'discipline of the secret' was a part of the early Church's life devoted to nurturing the knowledge of God and Christian character in committed disciples.[9] Such discipling was arcane or mysterious because it was not open to the merely curious or the general inquirer. This was because the early Christians recognized that discipleship can be distorted and misdirected by those who are not disciples; they understood that true discipleship is too important to the on-going life of the Church to risk this possibility.

Recovering and developing such disciplines are important for forming people to become wise readers of Scripture. In particular, such disciplines are important because we need to learn how closely our character and our witness are linked to our use of language. After all, Scripture tells the story of God calling forth a world, through the Word, where both humanity and God would dwell. As people who seek to structure our lives in accordance with this narrative of God's Word, we ought to place a very high value on the disciplined use of words in forming our lives and our witness. As Lash has suggested:

> Commissioned as ministers of God's redemptive Word, we are required, in politics and private life, in work and play, in commerce and scholarship, to practise and foster that philology, that word-caring, that meticulous and conscientious concern for the quality of conversation and the truthfulness of memory, which is the first casualty of sin. The Church, accordingly, is or should be a school of philology, an academy of word-care.[10]

Learning to become wise readers of Scripture requires, then, that we have the kind of character that enables us to be disciplined in our use of words.

Becoming disciplined in our use of words, however, also requires us to become wise readers of Scripture. As Augustine suggested, a person 'speaks more or less wisely to the extent that he has become more or less proficient in the Holy Scriptures'.[11] And, as Augustine further notes, we seek not only to read and speak wisely but also eloquently. We not only want to instruct ourselves and others in wise readings of Scripture, we also want to persuade ourselves and others so that the words we use may move us to more faithful living before God.[12]

Because our lives are to be patterned in relation to the One confessed in Scripture to be the Word incarnate, we need to be more than simply disciplined in our use of words; we need also to be disciplined by the Word made flesh. Being disciplined by the Word entails allowing our lives to be patterned in Christ. As such, we are to have a character that reflects neither that egocentric reading and witness in which God gets (at best) second-billing, nor that faceless reading and witness in which it is presumed that the messenger is irrelevant to the message. Rather, it involves a willingness to have our lives formed and transformed in and through particular Christian communities so that the words we use become means of pointing to the Word whom we follow.

Thus we need to participate in the friendships and practices of Christian communities in order to become wise readers of Scripture who can link the words we use with the Word whom we follow. As we have already suggested, this is not simply a general claim about the importance of community. We are called into such communities by the Triune God to whom the scriptural texts bear witness. Hence Christian communities provide the contexts whereby we learn – as the body of Christ through the power of the Holy Spirit – to interpret, and to have our lives interrogated by, the scriptural texts such that we are formed and transformed in the moral judgement necessary for us to live faithfully before God.

Making this case requires that we indicate more fully how and why the formation and transformation of our character is intimately connected to readings of Scripture in Christian communities that have been called into being by the Triune God.

## GOD, CHRISTIAN COMMUNITIES, AND SCRIPTURE

As we have already noted, Christians' complicity in sin prevents us from being disciplined in our language, judging righteously, and living well. Upon entering the body of Christ, Christians are to rely on their brothers and sisters to help each other recognize and overcome those features of our lives which undermine and frustrate our use of language, our judgement and our desire to live faithfully before God. Christian communities are the occasions in which, in the context of the 'dangerous' remembrance of Christ's passion, believers are enabled by Christ's resurrection to converse about how faithfully to live before the Triune God.[13]

The conversations and practices of Christian communities help to liberate us from our sin, enabling us to judge righteously. Nevertheless, we should not be surprised to find that Christian communities will often be puzzled about how best to understand their own existence and character in relation to the Triune God. Such puzzlements are found in the Scriptures themselves. After all, Paul reminds us that this side of the Kingdom we see in a mirror, dimly; only in the Kingdom will we see face to face (1 Cor. 13. 12). More generally, the biblical narrative *both* tells the story of the Triune God, focused in the life, death, and resurrection of Jesus of Nazareth, *and* displays the puzzlement of particular communities seeking to discern the significance of that story for their own existence and character.

There is a close link between the claims made on our lives by the Triune God and the shape of the particular communities in which we seek to become wise readers of Scripture. The interpretation of Scripture as an activity of communal discernment – the conversation in the good which is both formative and transformative and involves both destruction and construction of identities – is enabled by the Holy Spirit through Christ's resurrection. Communal discernment also provides the contexts for learning the judgements and rules by which Christians ascertain how we ought to live and what we ought to do.

Thus Christian communities are central for the ongoing task of enabling people to become wise readers of Scripture. To become wise readers of Scripture, we need to acquire a range of skills and virtues manifested in Christian discipleship. These skills and virtues are given their shape and form under the guidance of the Holy Spirit in and through the particular friendships and practices of Christian communities. They both are the prerequisite for, and the result of, wise readings of Scripture. These skills and virtues not only enable wise reading but faithful practice. They show forth a witness to God's ways with the world.

Even so, it may be objected that despite our criticisms of other writers on the Bible and ethics, our own account is truncated. After all, we have not discussed either how we should learn to read Scripture in Christian communities or the relationship between our readings of Scripture in the Church and other people's readings of the Bible (particularly in the academy). Moreover, we have not discussed what role Scripture ought to have in relation to other possible sources of ethical insight and wisdom.

We have not done so because there is no way to formulate these questions, much less answer them, outside of the particular contexts and situations in which Christians find themselves. Even so, we can indicate some of the ways in which we think such issues ought to be addressed. We do so in the next two sections.

## READINGS OF THE TEXTS

We have argued that Christian communities are constituted and reconstituted politically by Scripture, because Scripture provides the primary context for understanding what it means to live faithfully before God. Thus Christian communities must engage in 'readings of the texts'. By that we mean not only that we should provide readings of the texts that comprise the Scriptures, but also that we need to allow these texts to provide readings of our lives.[14]

However, we have not yet adequately explicated our understanding of the texts of which we should provide readings and allow to provide readings of us. Towards the end of Chapter 1 we made some comments about the status of the Bible as the Church's Scripture. We also noted that as Scripture the Bible provides the Church with a canon, a normative standard for the faith, practice and worship of Christian communities. Since throughout this book we distinguish between the Bible and the Church's Scripture, we need to explicate this difference and its relevance to learning to become wise readers of Scripture.

Part of the ethos of academic exegesis is the presumption that the Bible is simply one text that a scholar may study. Within the academy one scholar's comments about a Biblical text are of the same logical status as another scholar's comments about a Shakespearean sonnet. To be admitted to the guild of professional biblical scholars one need not (some would say should not) have any particular predisposition towards the Bible other than the conviction that it is a text about which one can say numerous interesting things.

When the Church, however, calls that same Bible its Scripture, or recognizes the Bible as its canon, it immediately places itself in a different relationship to the Bible than the academy has. When the Church calls the Bible its Scripture it not only assumes that the Bible is a text about which Christians can say many interesting things, the Church also claims that this text has provided and still provides the basis for Christian communities' ongoing struggle to live faithfully before God. When the Church recognizes the Old and New Testaments as its canon it means that these texts are the norm or rule to which we will conform our faith, practice and worship.[15] The Bible, then, as Scripture or canon forms the life of Christian communities in ways far different and more comprehensive than the Bible (as a text around which interested interpreters congregate) forms the academy of professional exegetes.

To emphasize the Bible's significance as the Church's Scripture or canon, however, invites misunderstanding due to the rather acrimonious debates in recent years over 'canonical criticism' and the 'canonical approach'.[16] Clearly, we cannot adjudicate all of these debates. We can, however, try to explain and to qualify our use of the term 'canon' in ways that will limit misunderstanding if not disagreement.

First, it is quite common to use canon to refer to a fixed list of books. According to this usage, the Christian canon is a list of books that was largely in place by the end of the second century and was finalized by the middle of the fourth century. Clearly, this is a coherent use of the term; it is simply not the way we are using the term in reference to the place of Scripture in Christian ethics. We think the significance of the canon for understanding Scripture in Christian ethics is as a norm, a standard of judgement. Both canon as norm and canon as list are acceptable ways of using the term. Failure to be precise about how one is using the term, however, can lead to confusion.

For example, using 'canon' to refer to a fixed list, one would have to admit that the earliest Christians did not have a canon. The fixing of a list was a later historical development. According to our use of canon, however, one would have to say that the earliest Christian communities recognized some texts and traditions as the norm to which their faith, practice and worship were to conform. We cannot completely specify the contours of that canon. Neither is it likely that all the earliest Christian communities agreed on the precise contours of the canon.[17] Without doubt, however, the Old Testament (probably in Greek) and a host of more or less formalized traditions about the life, death, and resurrection of Jesus would have been the basis for the standard to which the earliest Christian communities sought to conform their common life. This, at least, is what Paul seems to have presupposed in his own writings to these communities.

All communities that seek to form people so they will live faithful lives must have at least relatively formalized standards against which to judge what is faithful and what is not. It is not at all problematic to call that standard a canon. That standard for Christian communities is Scripture. To sustain this claim Christians need not believe that God dictated the text of the Bible to faithful scribes in ancient times. We do, however, need to have a view of Providence. Christian convictions about the canonical status of Scripture are sustained by a faith that the God who has called us to be the Church would not leave us bereft of the resources we need to follow that call faithfully.

Neither do Christians need to be surprised that those preceding them in the faith revised the shape and content of their canon in the light of their changing circumstances. Even if we cannot trace the rationale for, nor the exact shape of, these changes, critical biblical scholarship has persuasively shown that such processes were at work in earlier communities of believers. Those who seek to be wise readers of Scripture may well benefit from knowing about these various stages of the reception of the texts of the Bible. Christian communities must remember, however, that it is the present form of the text of the Bible that is canonical for them.[18] Christian communities conform their life and practice to the present form of their Scripture and not to J or E or to L or Q.[19]

Such convictions, however, need not limit the types of readings of Scripture which Christian communities might provide. Long before the rise of critical scholarship Christians gave a rich variety of faithful readings and embodiments of Scripture without the benefit of source, form, or redaction criticism. They used the diversity within the canon to their advantage, reading various texts in the light of others.[20]

There are manifold ways in which this has been and can be legitimately done. For example, difficult passages in Scripture about the place of women might be read in the light of Jesus's ministries to women *and* their ministries to him or in the light of Galatians 3.27–29.[21] Likewise, passages in the Old Testament may well be read 'directionally' through Jesus and Paul.[22] But there is no *a priori* way of knowing which texts can and/or should be used in any particular situations or interpretations. Practical wisdom, learned in and through particular Christian communities, is the means by which the appropriate texts and their interpretations are discerned.[23]

Our claims about the canonical shape of Scripture should not lead Christians to forsake critical biblical scholarship as it is carried out in the academy. Clearly, not all critical interests and activities are at all times equally relevant to any particular community. Nor do all people need to become critical biblical scholars. Yet the exercise of 'critical virtues' as nurtured in university departments and professional societies are important to the Church for a variety of reasons. For example, as we have already suggested, such critical virtues enable us to analyze textual traditions in order to discern the final form of the text. They enable linguistic skills for discerning how best to translate particular texts.

Secondly, critical scholarship can remind contemporary Christian communities that they are not the first people to desire to walk faithfully with Yahweh. Communities today stand within a Christian tradition that extends back beyond the time when the contours of our present Scripture were stabilized. We cannot escape being situated in such a tradition, nor should we wish to escape. Our predecessors in the faith, both Jewish and Christian, have asked questions, found answers, formulated texts and given readings of those texts which provide us with resources for our own lives. We cannot hope to become wise readers of Scripture in isolation from these resources in the tradition.

Further, critical scholarship can provide us with descriptions, analyses and interpretations of these various stages and various conflicts in the Christian tradition.[24] This is so both in terms of socio-historical awareness of the contexts in which particular writings were formed and received during the formation of the canon and in terms of the subsequent histories of how the texts have been interpreted by previous generations as well as other contemporaneous communities. The results of such critical practices serve as the long term memory of contemporary Christian communities. A critic in the service of such communities will use that memory to help shape both the interests a community brings to the reading of its canonical texts and the results of such interested readings.

In general, the exercise of critical virtues can help Christian communities withstand their tendencies to self-deception in the reading of Scripture. Such self-deception takes many forms, but it is generally based on the presumption that we today are the only ones who have heard the word of the Lord, that ours is the only true interpretation.

Ironically, some contemporary critical biblical scholars fall into this trap by presuming that they can deliver to us *the* meaning of the text apart from and despite thousands of years of interpretation and embodiment. Divested of any pretensions to deliver the meaning of the text, the practices of critical biblical scholarship are important to the ongoing life of Christian communities. Even so, by characterizing the importance of critical biblical scholarship in terms of critical *virtues* we want to emphasize that this task involves the interdependence of people with well-formed character in particular communities, not the dependence on experts which has so often rendered non-professional interpreters irrelevant.

There is at least one further reason why Christian communities committed to reading the final canonical form of their Scripture will always want to engage in critical biblical scholarship. While such communities believe God would not leave the people of God without the resources they need to live in a manner faithful to God's call, they also need to recognize that the Bible did not fall complete from the mouth of God. Individuals and communities over time performed the tasks needed to form the Scriptures. In this process of formation, which is itself an act of interpretation, various interests were brought to bear on the final shaping of this text. Those interests include not only serving the needs of the people of God but also preserving the status of one's own social group, class, or gender.

Recently, for example, the socio-historical analyses of Norman Gottwald in regard to the Hebrew Bible and Elizabeth Schüssler Fiorenza's feminist reconstructions of early Christianity have brought this point home.[25] While many scholars have questioned the actual details of either Gottwald's or Schüssler Fiorenza's accounts, their work has been important because they raise issues about the types of interests brought to bear on the formation/ interpretation of the texts which comprise the Christian canon.

It would be a mistake, however, to suggest that the texts themselves are distorted. Such a claim presupposes that there is some undistorted, neutral text against which other forms are judged to be distorted. We need to recognize that whenever people engage in writing or reading texts, they do so from particular standpoints and with particular interests. However, those need not be the standpoints and interests that subsequent readers adopt. The importance of critical biblical scholarship of the sort done by Gottwald and Schüssler Fiorenza should make Christians aware of the impact of issues such as power, class and gender in the formation/interpretation of the texts which comprise the Christian canon. This awareness is important if subsequent readers are not to find themselves simply replicating and adopting those standpoints and interests.

Indeed, the recognition that we all write and read texts with particular interests in mind can help contemporary readers to adopt strategies for interpreting Scripture that will expose and challenge influential presumptions about such issues as power, class, and gender.[26] The history of Scriptural interpretation shows that the canon provides a wealth of material for readings, particularly focused on the narratives of Jesus Christ in the Gospels, which can subvert any particular community's sedimented interpretations and performances.

Christian communities must be aware of the possibilities of interpreting Scripture in such a way that it supports rather than subverts corrupt and sinful practices. This means that we Christians will need to learn to read the Scriptures 'over-against ourselves' rather than simply 'for ourselves'.[27] This is the sense in which our 'readings of the texts' involve allowing the texts to provide readings of us. In later chapters we will comment in more detail about reading 'over-against ourselves' as we find examples of doing such reading (in the life of Dietrich Bonhoeffer) and examples of failing to do such reading (The Dutch Reformed Church in South Africa).

Our ability or our failure to read Scripture 'over-against ourselves' can have significant consequences for our day to day struggle to live faithfully before God. Nevertheless, there is no method to guarantee that we will read 'over-against ourselves'. There are, however, at least two rules of thumb that can help us read 'over-against ourselves'. First, we must be willing to be interrogated *by* Scripture in addition to interrogating Scripture.[28] Of course, since Scripture does not actually talk, Scripture's interrogatory power will come to any community through the voices of interpreters with well-formed character within the community and concerned outsiders.[29]

Scripture interrogates us in manifold ways. For example, as we have already noted, we come to Scripture with particular predispositions, ideologies and theological presumptions. Left unchallenged, we will fail to recognize the corrupting power of these predispositions, ideologies and theological presumptions. The interrogatory power of Scripture challenges us to be constantly reforming the preconceptions we inevitably bring to interpretation.[30] For example, the biblical identification of 'God is love' has yielded a popular picture in middle-class America that God is a 'therapeutic nice-guy'. This picture needs to be challenged by such texts as Amos where God demands repentance and justice rather than prescribes therapy.

Further, allowing ourselves to be interrogated by Scripture entails a willingness to struggle with difficult and/or obscure texts. But of course there is no *a priori* way to know what texts we will find difficult or obscure. For example, middle-class British and North American Christians may find the story of the rich young ruler very difficult (Mark 10.17–22 and parallels), and followers and sympathizers of Rudolf Bultmann may find particular miracle stories or apocalyptic texts difficult unless they are demythologized. In the context of South African oppression, Allan Boesak has found the injunction of Jesus to forgive others not seven times but seventy times seven (Matt. 18.21–22 and parallel) – a passage many middle-class people in Britain and North America seemingly take for granted – to be an extraordinarily difficult passage. And yet, even though this passage is not particularly suited to his own desires, he allows the text to interrogate him.

Boesak asks, 'Is it possible to transcend our present situation in South Africa? Can it still happen? I do not know. I do not know how to tell the Blacks in South Africa to forgive seventy times seven times – those who have seen their own children shot and killed in the streets. I do not know how to tell them this.' He insists that in such a context people ought not speak too hastily about forgiveness and such matters. 'And yet,' he continues, 'we read these words of the Lord, words that we cannot avoid. Ought we to believe that what is impossible for us is possible for God? With God all things are possible, including forgiveness welling up out of the hearts of suffering and oppressed Black South Africans. That too. Precisely that.'[31] Boesak provides an important example of how and why we not only should interrogate texts but also ought to allow texts which we find difficult (for one reason or another) to interrogate us.[32]

A second rule of thumb for learning to read 'over-against ourselves' is that, as we have already suggested, such ability can be enhanced by ongoing engagements with critical scholarship on the part of contemporary Christian communities. We are not claiming that all Christians must become biblical scholars in order to read Scripture well. Rather, in order that communities can embody wise readings of Scripture, they need to nurture and develop people who are capable of exercising the critical virtues of professional biblical scholarship.

What we did not mention earlier, and need to point out here, is that it will cost communities something to take seriously this responsibility of nurturing and developing people skilled in the application of critical biblical scholarship. For, as Ben Sira notes in the deutero-canonical book Ecclesiasticus, 'The wisdom of the scholar depends on the opportunity of leisure and someone who has little business may become wise' (38.24ff.). One does not become skilled as a critical exegete without the time to be fully devoted to that task. That time comes from being relieved of other duties. Others will have to pick up this slack if Christian communities are serious about nurturing biblical scholars. There is always a possibility that people in the community will resent this burden, especially if they don't see how the scholar is helping the community. In addition, there is a tremendous temptation to arrogance on the part of the would-be scholar.[33] Hence, communities must recognize these possibilities and choose people wisely for the task of scholarship.

Would-be scholars from any particular Christian communities, for their part, must remember the cost to the communities that set them apart for a specific task. Consequently, they must remember that such a task is a work of service to those communities. Only would-be scholars who develop and retain the humility that this perspective demands will be able to handle faithfully the divided allegiances that will necessarily develop when they become fully fledged members of the scholarly community as well as members of particular Christian communities. In times of conflict between these allegiances, such scholars must remember that their primary allegiance is to the God who is worshipped in and through particular Christian communities. This allegiance to God must ultimately determine scholars' practice.

Throughout this section we have been arguing for the importance of providing 'readings of the texts'. We have understood that both in terms of the need for us to read the texts that comprise the Christian canon and in terms of the importance of allowing the texts to provide readings of us. We still need to address how Scripture is related both to the various contexts in which we live and to other possible sources for ethical guidance.

## READINGS OF THE WORLD

We have argued that Scripture is best read in and through Christian communities. Such communities, however, find themselves within the political arrangements of wider societies. They need to understand these larger contexts and the ways in which they impinge on Christian communities if Christians' readings of Scripture are to enable them to live faithfully. Hence faithful interpretation requires not only 'readings of the texts' but also 'readings of the world'. In a manner analogous to our argument about 'readings of the texts', believers need to provide readings of the world and also to allow the world to provide readings of us and of the politics of our communities.

It is important to provide readings of the world for at least three interrelated reasons. First, using a more restricted sense of the notion 'world' than found in ordinary usage, we need to call the world to account for its unbelief. This sense of the 'world', derived from particular biblical passages, refers to all that which is opposed to God. So the Letter of James, for example, suggests that one who seeks to be a friend of the 'world' puts himself at enmity with God (Jas. 4.4).[34] Likewise in John's Gospel Jesus is quoted as saying that '[the world] hates me because I testify against it that its works are evil' (John 7.7, NRSV). In this sense, providing a reading of the world entails calling to account all those who continue to be in rebellion against God. But the only ways in which we can call them to account is first to understand what they are about.

Secondly, Christians need to provide readings of the world because the world remains a part of God's good creation *to* which God sent Jesus Christ and *in* which Christians are to serve (see John 17.15–19). The scope of God's work, particularly as focused in Jesus of Nazareth, remains the world.[35] This world is not simply a spiritual abstraction. Rather, it is an arena of social, economic, and political interactions, conflicts and cooperative endeavours. In particular, then, we need to discern and describe well the material conditions in which we find ourselves. No situation in which Christians (either now or in the past) find themselves is self-interpreting. The process of faithfully embodying an interpretation of Scripture presupposes that Christian communities have already analysed and diagnosed the contexts in which they find themselves. Such analysis must be informed and directed by Scripture, but it is not simply an interpretation of Scripture.

In part our argument has to do with the now familiar claims about the importance of the 'social location' of the interpreter.[36] It makes a difference whether one is interpreting Scripture in the barrios of Los Angeles or the Houses of Parliament in Westminster, and we need to be aware of that difference. Nevertheless, diagnosing the material conditions in which we find ourselves goes beyond claims about social location. We need to analyse the ways in which the wider societies in which we live construct our identities and our relations with one another.

So, for example, in the contexts of modern Western societies, people's readings of the world ought to be informed by analyses of such features of contemporary life as individualism, consumerism, bureaucracy, reliance on managerial expertise, and the politics of our discursive practices.[37] These readings entail complex moral, political, economic, social-psychological and historical issues. We need to consider, learn from, and also criticize sources and resources other than Scripture which address both the tasks of ethics and particular moral issues. For example, if we are addressing the problems of hunger in the world, we will need to utilize the resources of economic analyses as well as international politics. Or if we are addressing issues of medicine, we will need to draw on the resources of contemporary scientific investigations. We may also need to turn to the perspectives of other religious traditions in discerning approaches to moral questions or to an issue like the environment. If Christians' readings of Scripture for Christian ethics are to be wise, then we need to discern as wisely as possible the actual material conditions in which we find ourselves and the ways in which those conditions impinge not only on us but on others around the world.

We are contending that Scripture is the primary source and norm for Christian ethics. Thus our readings of the world should not be simply correlated with our readings of the texts as if each carries equal status in Christian ethical discernment. This is the danger of seeking to establish *methods* for relating Scripture to other sources and resources of moral guidance. The priority of readings of the texts does not in any way preclude drawing on other sources and resources. Indeed we are convinced that wise readings of the texts for Christian ethics actually *requires* that we provide readings of the world. But that conviction can too easily be misunderstood, and so we offer two caveats.

First, we need to recognize that Christians often disagree with one another about how best to read the world. We can and do need to learn from conversation and argument with fellow Christians. Further, Christians can and do need to learn from people in other disciplines and with other interests. When we do so, however, we need to remember that their readings of the world, whether in relation to economic analyses, moral judgements, or political calculations, are *not* descriptively neutral. We should not see them as neutral experts. Rather they are themselves providing readings from which we can learn and that we ought also to evaluate critically.

The second caveat is a reminder of something that we have already suggested, only this time with a different emphasis. Earlier we indicated that readings of the world ought to be informed by Scripture, but they are not themselves interpretations of Scripture. Now we need to emphasize the former part of that claim. Even when we are providing readings of the world, those readings ought to be informed and guided by our readings of Scripture. The ways we describe ourselves and the situations we face (much less the world) are matters of controversy. Because of this, we need to remember that Scripture provides the primary context for our descriptions and the way we learn to make those descriptions.

One might object that there are numerous ethical issues that we face about which Scripture is silent. We will say more about this supposed 'gap' later. For now, let us note that while this is true, the force of the objection is overstated. Even where Scripture is silent in terms of any direct address to a moral issue, we can and ought to work analogically from the descriptions of Scripture to our descriptions and evaluations of particular concrete issues.[38]

While these reasons indicate why we need to provide readings of the world, we need also to learn to allow the world to provide readings of us. That might seem odd, given our convictions about the centrality of providing readings of the texts. The world does not retain an independent authority over-against Scripture in discerning how we ought to live. Our primary task is learning to live faithfully before the Triune God by embodying the Scriptures. Even so, however, the world's readings of us present challenges as well as insights that can assist us in learning to live as scriptural people. This is so for several reasons.

First, in our judgement of the world we also judge ourselves. We discover the ways in which our own lives, as communities and individuals, continue to reflect that 'world' of unbelief rather than the Gospel of Jesus Christ. As James Wm. McClendon has suggested, 'the line between church and world passes right through each Christian's heart'.[39] We need to allow the world to provide readings of us because we can too easily conflate the

Church and the Kingdom, presuming that the world is not – or at least is not any longer – a part of our lives. So, for example, when we condemn racism or sexism as incompatible with the Gospel of Jesus Christ, we need to allow the world to 'read' us by showing how the practices and institutions of Christian communities continue to be racist and sexist.

A second reason we need to allow the world to provide readings of us is because the material conditions in which we live not only shape our societies but shape our Christian communities in ways that are incompatible with Christian convictions. Christian communities too often and too easily reflect the material conditions of our societies and our culture instead of manifesting alternative ways of ordering common life. Christian communities in modern Western societies are beset by such problems as individualism, bureaucratic rationality and consumerism. Hence, the analyses of social theorists are important not only for diagnosing the conditions in which we live but also for critically evaluating the practices and institutions of Christian communities and Christian lives.

Third, we also need to see what other disciplines and other readings of the world, including other religions, have to teach us. Other sources and resources of moral guidance contain wisdom from which we can enhance our own understandings of what it means to live faithfully before God. As Augustine puts it:

> In the same way all the teachings of the pagans contain not only simulated and superstitious imaginings and grave burdens of unnecessary labor, which each one of us leaving the society of pagans under the leadership of Christ ought to abominate and avoid, but also liberal disciplines more suited to the uses of truth, and some most useful precepts concerning morals. Even some truths concerning the worship of one God are discovered among them.[40]

We need to be open to the discovery of wisdom wherever it can be discerned.

Nevertheless, we need to pay attention to that wisdom's congruence with our readings of the scriptural texts. We sometimes mistake cultural presumptions and societal fads for divine wisdom. Once again, there is no way to guarantee an adequate resolution of these issues in advance. As we have repeatedly insisted, there is no substitute for practical wisdom. That is, learning how to hold together readings of the texts and readings of the world is a lifelong project to be carried out in and through communities formed and transformed by the Holy Spirit.

Archbishop Oscar Romero's life and death provide an excellent example of someone who, through his participation in Christian communities, learned to embody Christian practical wisdom. He learned how to hold together powerful readings of both Scripture and the world. Romero was appointed Archbishop of San Salvador in 1977 because he was considered to be politically safe. Yet over the next three years Romero developed powerful readings both of the biblical texts and of the world that were anything but politically safe.[41] Romero did not develop these readings in isolation; they emerged from worshipping, conversing and living among fellow Christians, particularly poor Salvadorans who gathered together for worship and study in 'base Christian communities'. These readings led him to speak out prophetically against the spiral of violence that was ravaging El Salvador.[42] An assassin finally silenced Romero's voice on 24 March 1980 as he celebrated Holy Communion. Even so, the wisdom of Romero's readings, as embodied in his life and death, has enabled many people – both in El Salvador and beyond – to understand more clearly the interconnections between readings of the texts and readings of the world.

## CONCLUSION

In this chapter we have argued that the interpretation of Scripture is a difficult task *not* because of the technical demands of biblical scholarship but because of the importance of character for wise readings. We pointed to the importance of Christian communities that are given their shape and form by the Triune God as the central contexts for learning to be wise readers of Scripture. We further suggested that in and through those Christian communities we need to engage both readings of the texts and readings of the world. Throughout, we have insisted on the importance of practical wisdom for both interpreting Scripture and discerning how we ought to live and what we ought to do.

Even though many people might acknowledge the importance of practical wisdom and Christian communities for understanding the place of Scripture in Christian ethics, there is still likely to be considerable uneasiness about staking too much on such notions. After all, we have not yet addressed the discontinuities between Scripture and our own contemporary settings. Isn't what we have argued for in these first two chapters undermined, or at least relativized, by the problems of bridging the gap between the first-centuries of the common era (when the Christian canon was formed) and the late twentieth?

Moreover, do we really want to place so much emphasis on Christian communities given the ways in which people can become alienated from and/or marginalized by those communities? And how can we cope with the conflicts and fractured character not only within communities but among diverse and competing Christian communities? Have we failed to acknowledge the importance of individual believers in the midst of an emphasis on community?

We do not think that such questions are unanswerable or raise insuperable problems for our position. They do, however, call for further explication. To that task we turn in Chapter 3.

## NOTES

1. For a more extended discussion of the importance of formation and transformation in moral judgement, and a discussion from which we have drawn considerably in what follows, see L. Gregory Jones, *Transformed Judgment: Toward a Trinitarian Account of the Moral Life* (Notre Dame, IN: University of Notre Dame Press, 1990), particularly Chapter 3.

2. Practical wisdom, a notion that goes back to Aristotle, is the virtue of knowing how appropriately to discern a situation and to enact that discernment. The need for practical wisdom arises with questions that do not admit of demonstration. Ethics is one of those areas, and so is interpretation.

3. Nicholas Lash, *Theology on the Way to Emmaus* (London: SCM, 1986), p. 54.

4. ibid., p. 55.

5. See George Lindbeck, *The Nature of Doctrine* (London, SPCK; Philadelphia, PA: Westminster, 1984), pp. 117–18.

6. This is Stanley Hauerwas's suggested revision of the claim that Scripture 'creates' a world in his *A Community of Character* (Notre

Dame, IN: University of Notre Dame Press, 1981), p. 57.

7. See Chapter 4 for a further development of the interrelations between character and interpretive skill.

8. As we will show in Chapter 6, this is a lesson that Dietrich Bonhoeffer learned and reflected on in the midst of Nazi Germany.

9. We take the phrase 'discipline of the secret' from Dietrich Bonhoeffer. In his *Letters and Papers from Prison*, Bonhoeffer reflected, albeit briefly and somewhat cryptically, on the importance of recovering the early church's *disciplina arcana* for contemporary Christian life and witness. We think Bonhoeffer's judgement is important. We describe Bonhoeffer's views in relation to his life in Chapter 6, and our own understanding of the importance of such a discipline for contemporary life is developed further in Chapter 3.

10. Nicholas Lash, 'Ministry of the Word or Comedy and Philology', *New Blackfriars* 68 (1987), pp. 476–77.

11. Augustine, *On Christian Doctrine*, tr. D. W. Robertson Jr (New York: Macmillan, 1958), p. 122.

12. For an extended discussion of the rhetorical character of Christian theology in general and the interpretation of Scripture in particular, see the Ph.D. dissertation of David S. Cunningham, 'Faithful Persuasion: Prolegomena to a Rhetoric of Christian Theology' (Duke University, 1990).

13. The notion of the 'dangerous' memory of Jesus Christ is taken from Johann Baptist Metz, *Faith in History and Society: Toward a Practical Fundamental Theology*, tr. David Smith (New York: Crossroad, 1980).

14. For this idea of phrasing our readings in a systematically ambiguous way, we are indebted to Rowan Williams's argument with reference to the 'judgement of the world' in his 'Postmodern Theology and the Judgment of the World', in *Postmodern Theology*, ed. Frederic B. Burnham (New York: Harper and Row, 1989), pp. 92–112.

15. It seems that Christians are almost always in the dangerous position of forgetting the significance of the presence of the Old Testament in the Christian Canon. If the Church is to see itself as people of the God of Abraham, Deborah, Moses and Jesus (as it should), then the Old Testament will always be of abiding importance for faithful living. The question of how any particular Christian community will manifest the importance of the Old Testament in any particular situation is an open one. This is particularly true in regard to the Old Testament's relationship to the New Testament. There is no context-independent way to specify the relationship between the Old and New Testaments.

16. The term 'canonical criticism' is most closely associated with the work of James A. Sanders. See particularly *Torah and Canon* (Philadelphia, PA: Fortress, 1972) and *Canon and Community: A Guide to Canonical Criticism* (Philadelphia, PA: Fortress, 1984). The term 'canonical approach' is often used to describe the somewhat different proposals of Brevard Childs. Childs has been developing his

position over the last 35 years. The best examples of his views are presented in *Introduction to the Old Testament as Scripture* (London: SCM, 1979); *The New Testament as Canon: An Introduction* (London: SCM, 1984) and *Old Testament Theology in a Canonical Context* (London: SCM, 1985). Childs's most persistent if not perspicacious critic has been James Barr. See particularly *Holy Scripture: Canon, Authority, Criticism* (Oxford: Oxford University Press, 1983). The most sympathetic reconstruction of Childs' position can be found in Mark Brett's forthcoming book *Biblical Criticism in Crisis?* (Cambridge: Cambridge University Press).

17. Even today, the contours of the Christian canon vary to some degree depending on whether one is Roman Catholic, Orthodox or Protestant. It is not clear to us, however, that this is a major problem. Without doubt there are large differences between these Christian groups. Some of these differences are due to interpretive disputes. Nevertheless, these differences generally (with a few possible exceptions) do not seem to depend on the shape of any particular group's canon. Important issues do need to be addressed within ecumenical contexts about how we ought to construe 'Scripture' in these various traditions.

    Even in ecumenical discussions, however, we ought not over-emphasize the differences. One would need to show how a concrete dispute hinges on differences over the shape of the Christian canon before we allow these differences to become too prominent in discussions of Scripture's place in Christian ethics. When such a case arises, such as the reference to 'purgatory' in Second Maccabees, it will have to be resolved in conversation among the various parties (as with all ecumenical disputes).

18. This does not eliminate the issues raised by textual criticism about how we discern what is the 'final form' of the text. To take a well-known example, does the Gospel of Mark properly end at 16.8 or 16.20? Such questions are important, but they do not undermine the notion of reading the 'final form' of the text. Rather, as we will suggest below, these questions point to the importance of developing critical virtues that will enable us to discern wisely how to construe the final form.

19. See also the comments of Charles Wood: 'It is, for example, the book of Exodus or the Gospel of Matthew which is canonically decisive, and not the various strands, strata, and sources of tradition which may lie behind either and which might be reconstructed as oral or written "works" in their own right. This does not mean that historical considerations are irrelevant to a canonical reading of the texts. Historical awareness of the ways in which a given writing was perceived and read at the time of the formation of the Christian canon may provide crucial insight into its canonical significance, while the history of its subsequent interpretation may well be relevant to one's own attempts at canonical exegesis'. *The Formation of Christian Understanding* (Philadelphia, PA: Westminster, 1981), p. 92.

20. For examples of how this was done in early Christianity, see Rowan Greer's discussion in James L. Kugel and Rowan A. Greer, *Early Biblical Interpretation* (Philadelphia, PA: Westminster, 1986), pp. 107–203; for examples from medieval Christianity, see Beryl Smalley, *Study of the Bible in the Middle Ages* (Oxford: Basil Blackwell; Notre Dame, IN: University of Notre Dame Press, 1964).

21. See, for example, Letty Russell, *Household of Freedom* (Philadelphia, PA: Westminster, 1987). See also our comments on the story of the Syro-Phoenician woman in Chapter 5.

22. See the comment by John Howard Yoder on 'the believers' church' heritage: 'Instead of a timeless collection of parabolic anecdotes for allegorical exposition, the Bible is a story of promise and fulfillment which must be read directionally. The New Testament, by affirming the Hebrew Scriptures which Christians have come to call the Old Testament, also interprets them. Abraham and Moses are read through Jesus and Paul', *The Priestly Kingdom*, p. 9.

23. Some might object that this practice sets up a canon within a canon, ultimately failing to take seriously the canon as it stands now. Within a canon as diverse as the one Christians recognize, there is no reason to think that all of its texts will be equally relevant all of the time. Some texts will be more appropriate than others in any given situation. This sets up a 'functional' canon within the canon. But a 'functional' canon within the canon, discerned in the particular contexts of Christian communities, is considerably different from a 'normative' canon within the canon which *a priori* excludes some texts from consideration. We reject the notion of a normative canon within the canon. A functional one, however, is not a problem as long as Christians recognize that in a different context different texts may provide the basis for a faithful response. No text – no matter how 'difficult' – should be excluded from the ongoing processes of communal discernment in relation to the whole witness of Scripture.

24. The Christian tradition embodies continuities of conflict among different ecclesial groups (as well as within them) about how to construe the whole of Scripture as well as how to read particular texts of Scripture. Such conflicts have been and in many ways continue to be divisive. We are not convinced, however, that in many contemporary contexts differences in ecclesial traditions either are or ought to be predominant in understandings of the place of Scripture in Christian ethics. As we will suggest later in this chapter and in later chapters, the fact that many people today participate in more than one community of Christians has significantly altered the ways in which those people read and understand Scripture (see also Chapter 6 for examples of the ways in which Dietrich Bonhoeffer's trip to Rome, his participation with blacks in Harlem, and his contact with a French Calvinist who was a pacifist all had significant impacts on his readings of Scripture).

25. See Norman K. Gottwald, *The Tribes of Yahweh* (London: SCM, 1979) and Elizabeth Schüssler Fiorenza, *In Memory of Her: A Feminist Theological Reconstruction of Christian Origins* (London: New York: Crossroad, 1986). See also Itumeleng J. Mosala, *Biblical Hermeneutics and Black Theology in South Africa* (Grand Rapids, MI: Wm. B. Eerdmans, 1989).

26. See, for examples, Phyllis Trible, *Texts of Terror* (Philadelphia, PA: Fortress, 1984); Ched Myers, *Binding the Strong Man* (Maryknoll, NY: Orbis, 1988).

27. We borrow these terms from Dietrich Bonhoeffer, who develops them in his lecture 'The Presentation of New Testament Texts', in *No Rusty Swords*, tr. E. H. Robertson, et al. (London: Collins, 1970), pp. 302–20. See below, Chapter 6, for a discussion of this argument in the context of Bonhoeffer's own life.

28. See also J. D. G. Dunn and James P. Mackey, *New Testament Theology in Dialogue* (London: SPCK; Philadelphia, PA: Westminster, 1979), p. 6, where they note: 'At the same time we may well find that the New Testament writings do not merely answer back our questions. The New Testament may put *us* in question.'

29. See below, Chapters 4 and 5, for further discussions of both of these types of reader.

30. Many theological and political disputes within the Church are interminable because we don't want Scripture to interrogate us. But as David Kelsey has noted, there are also theological disputes about how to construe Scripture. See *The Uses of Scripture in Recent Theology* (Philadelphia, PA: Fortress, 1975). While it is important to recognize such theological disputes about how to construe Scripture, the focus ought not to be on the theological arguments but on how we ought to order our lives in relation to Scripture. Rowan Greer's comment about the early Church is instructive: 'For [the fathers of the early Church], Scripture yielded a theological vision when rightly interpreted. And theological disputes in the early Church were largely arguments about how rightly to describe that vision and to define the hero of the story that comprised the vision. Nevertheless, the theological vision did not exist for its own sake. It was meant to be translated into renewed human lives,' in Kugel and Greer, *Early Biblical Interpretation*, p. 195.

31. Allan Boesak, *Black and Reformed* (Maryknoll, NY: Orbis, 1984), pp. 155–6. We are indebted to Gerald West for directing us to this passage.

32. We noted earlier that different communities adopt functional 'canons within the canon' in providing readings of the texts. And we further suggested that such functional differences were not problematic so long as they were not allowed to become normative. Here we would note that, whereas different communities construct functional canons in their interpretation, we also need to allow the canon of Scripture to construct us. This would be the analogous move at

the canonical level to our claim about allowing particular texts to interrogate us.

33. Ben Sira also recognizes this and reflects on the importance of maintaining a proper relationship between scholars and craftspeople for the continuing health of a society. See particularly Ecclesiasticus 38.31–34.

34. See below, Chapter 3, for further discussion of this passage and its relation to the ways in which Christian communities should be related to wider societies.

35. See also below, Chapter 3.

36. Recall our discussion of the politics of interpretive interests in Chapter 1.

37. Many people have turned to such figures as Marx, Nietzsche and Freud for their readings of the world (understanding 'world' here in the context of modern Western societies), but to that list we might also add such (diverse and competing) theorists as Max Weber, Robert Bellah, Peter Berger, Michel Foucault, Jürgen Habermas, Julia Kristeva and Alasdair MacIntyre. Moreover, we ought also to remember that some of the most powerful readings of the world come from artists as diverse as Angela Carter, Don DeLillo, Spike Lee, and Walker Percy.

38. Medical ethics would seem to be one of those areas where Scripture is silent on many of the issues we are now facing. But, as Richard Mouw has suggested, that does not imply that Scripture should not play an important role in how we 'read' and describe the issues that are being raised. See 'Biblical Revelation and Medical Decisions', in Revisions, eds Stanley Hauerwas and Alasdair MacIntyre (Notre Dame, IN: University of Notre Dame Press, 1983), pp. 182–202.

39. James Wm. McClendon, Ethics: Systematic Theology Vol. I (Nashville, TN: Abingdon, 1986) p. 17.

40. Augustine, On Christian Doctrine, p. 75.

41. See, for examples of Romero's readings, The Violence of Love: The Pastoral Wisdom of Archbishop Oscar Romero, ed. James R. Brockman (New York: Harper and Row, 1988).

42. Jon Sobrino has emphasized Romero's prophetic role in his Archbishop Romero: Memories and Reflections, tr. Robert R. Barr (Maryknoll, NY: Orbis, 1990), especially pp. 101–66.

# 3

## Recovering a Common Life: Learning to Become People of Character

We have argued that in order to articulate adequately the place of Scripture in Christian ethics, we need to recover the centrality of the friendships and practices of Christian communities. We have further argued that this is not simply a general claim about the value of 'community'. Our claim arises out of the conviction that Scripture is addressed principally to communities constituted and reconstituted by the Triune God. Moreover, we have also claimed that the political constitution of the Church demands that Christians embody their interpretations of Scripture in their present situations. The aim of adopting any particular interpretive interest in regard to Scripture, so we are arguing, is that Scripture itself calls for the formation and reformation of communities of people living faithfully before the God of Jesus Christ.

At the end of Chapter 2 we discussed the importance of engaging both readings of the texts and readings of the world and specific ways of doing this. As we briefly noted in the last chapter, one might object that our discussion failed to confront the fact that there are vast discontinuities between Scripture and contemporary life. After all, perhaps the most enduring message of biblical scholars to the Church over the last fifty years is that the world of the Bible is immeasurably different from our own world. Christians cannot simply replicate a mirror image of first-century Christian communities. The diverse material situations of believers today are not those of Jesus, Prisca or Paul much less those of Abraham or Deborah. Thus faithful interpretation cannot simply be a matter of trying to recreate those conditions in the twentieth century.

This claim of biblical scholarship has often been understood as creating a difficult, and perhaps even insuperable, barrier for faithful reading of Scripture in the present. But our argument is that it need not. To be sure, there are important discontinuities between Scripture and our contemporary settings. But the discontinuities that arise from historical divergences are not nearly as important for faithful interpretation as are the discontinuities that arise from our contemporary failure to embody faithful living in ongoing Christian communities. That is, the discontinuities are not so much historical as moral and theological.

In this chapter we will first explain why the claim about historical discontinuities does not create as imposing a barrier as many people think. Secondly, we will explicate some of the problems raised by the moral discontinuities of our failure to embody faithful living. And finally, we will suggest how and why we need to recover the centrality of Christian communities if we are to embody faithful interpretation of Scripture for Christian life and ethics.

## BIBLICAL AND CONTEMPORARY COMMUNITIES

One of the most common ways of construing the discontinuities between Scripture and our contemporary settings is to posit a sharp distinction between what the text 'originally meant' and what the text 'now means today'.[1] In the first place, such a construal is deeply problematic. The formulation begs the question of 'meaning'.[2] Even more, the model reflects a problematic notion of how the past and the present are related. On this model the task of the biblical scholar is to find out what the text 'originally meant', and then, as if in a relay race, pass off the text to the contemporary theologian or ethicist to figure out what it should 'now mean today'.[3] But the model need not be, and in fact should not be, unidirectional.

In contrast, we argue that the relationship actually should be one of mutual dependence. As Nicholas Lash has put it:

> If it is true for us, as creatures of history, that some understanding of our past is a necessary condition of an accurate grasp of our present predicament and our responsibilities for the future, it is also true that a measure of critical self-understanding of our present predicament is a

necessary condition of an accurate 'reading' of our past. We do not *first* understand the past and *then* proceed to understand the present. The relationship between these two dimensions of our quest for meaning and truth is dialectical: they mutually inform, enable, correct, and enlighten each other.[4]

On this alternative view, the tension between the past and the present remains; there are historical discontinuities. This view, however, situates the tension between the past and the present differently. As a result, the tasks of interpretation are differently understood. Contrary to what has become standard practice in biblical studies, we do not begin by attempting to understand the past on its own terms and then ask about the past's present relevance.

This is because we do not begin from some neutral standpoint with either the past or the present. Since we are situated historically, there is no neutral standpoint from which we can see either our past or our present. Nor is there a neutral language we can use in describing either the past or the present. Therefore, we should not blithely assume unbroken continuity in the understandings of any particular notion. For example, the notion of 'justice' in Micah is considerably different from the notion of 'justice' in the American Pledge of Allegiance. That is why, as Lash suggests, we have to work analogically and dialectically between the past and the present to seek to find ways of appropriately connecting the patterns of human action.[5]

Indeed we find examples of this thinking in the practice of some of the earliest Christians as reflected in Scripture. While these believers did not have the *same* Scripture that we do today, they did have a canon – a formalized norm to which they struggled to make their faith and practice conform. This canon was constituted by traditions about the life, death and resurrection of Jesus Christ and by (what became known as) the Old Testament read in the light of their experience of the resurrected Christ. The common life of these earliest Christian communities can be seen as their attempt socially to embody their interpretations of this canon. Indeed, most of the New Testament documents, and the Pauline epistles in particular, were addressed to concrete communities engaged in this process of social embodiment.

Like Christians today, these believers could not simply replicate the life and practices of the people of Yahweh as described in the

Old Testament. Further, even though they were temporally much nearer the life of Jesus than we are, the different concrete setting in which they found themselves meant that they could not strictly replicate his life and practice. While the historical discontinuities between their canon and their communities were perhaps not as sharp as our own, the very presence of those discontinuities meant that there was a tension between the past and the present in their interpretive practices.

These believers, however, did not seem to be preoccupied by the historical discontinuities between their canon and their particular contexts. Rather, they tried imaginatively to formulate metaphors, draw analogies, and make connections between their canon and their present situations to order and adapt their common life in a manner appropriate to that canon. The crucial issues were moral and theological, not historical.

Two examples of these ways of negotiating the discontinuities can be found in Romans 6.1–11 and Philippians 1.27–2.18.[6] In Romans 6 Paul addresses the question 'Shall we remain in sin that grace might increase?' The question arises from Paul's comments in Romans 5. In answer to this question Paul employs a series of metaphors that tell, in an abbreviated form, the story of the change in political allegiance that occurs when one enters the Christian community. This entry provides the Christian with a new identity which makes the notion of 'remaining in sin' incoherent. At the same time, Paul notes, entry into the Christian community through baptism provides the believer with a logically self-involving commitment to do good and to be holy.

The metaphors Paul uses here to describe the change that occurs in the believer draw their force from their relationship to the story of the life, death and resurrection of Jesus Christ. Metaphors such as 'dying to sin' (Rom. 6.2), 'being baptized into Christ (and Christ's death)' (6.3), 'walking in newness of life' (6.4), and so forth are all tied either explicitly or implicitly to the story of Christ's person and work which must have constituted part of the canon of the earliest believers. Paul 'reads' this canon in such a way that it provides the community he is addressing with an understanding of how they are to live in their present situation. His reading aims not only to change the community's understanding, but to have its members embody this notion of dying to sin and walking in newness of life.

In Philippians 1.27ff. Paul addresses a community of believers who seem to be suffering some form of persecution (1.28–30). Paul at this point is concerned that these believers continue to 'walk worthily of the gospel of Christ' (1.27). In 2.1–4 he specifies particular forms of behaviour the Church is to practise. The force of these ethical demands is that if the Philippians are to walk in a manner worthy of the gospel of Christ in the face of opponents seeking their destruction, then they must remain steadfast in their faith, united in a selfless love and concern for one another. Such behaviour, while it will necessarily entail suffering, will result in their salvation (see 1.28).

All of these ethical demands are based on the poetic narration of Christ's activity in 2.6–11. Clearly, both Paul and the Philippians would have realized that no human could perfectly imitate this story about Christ. There cannot be a one-to-one relationship between the Christ–event narrated in 2.6–11 and the Philippians' situation. If the Philippians are to let the events presented in 2.6–11 guide their common life, they will have to draw an analogy from those events to their own situation.

This is what Paul has done in this section of the epistle. He has explicated the similarity-in-difference between the story of Christ in 2.6–11 that, in some form, would have been part of his (and the Philippians') canon, and the situation that the Philippians face. He has used this to support the view that God will vindicate the Philippians if they remain steadfast in their faith. To put the analogy crudely: if the Philippians will unite in a steadfast adherence to the gospel (which will entail the practice of the virtues related in 2.2–4), even in the face of suffering, then God will save them in the same way he saved the humiliated suffering Christ in verses 6–11. Paul's admonition in 2.5 is a call to recognize this, to apply to their communal life the precedent that is theirs by virtue of the fact that the Philippians are in Christ. Again, the validity of Paul's reading would have been confirmed as the Philippians embody the story of Christ related in 2.6–11 in the manner Paul proposes.

It is important to note, however, that there is no formulaic pattern to the types of readings Paul gives. He does not follow a method designed to yield meaning which he then applies to a particular situation. Rather, he interprets his canon in the light of the particular situation he is addressing. His interpretation would then be confirmed as the believers embody it in their particular social contexts. These brief comments about Paul are not designed to deny the numerous discontinuities between Scripture and our contemporary settings. Rather, these comments allow us to make two points about such discontinuities. First, as we have already argued, even the earliest Christians felt them. Temporal distance is not simply a problem of modernity.

Second, the most important discontinuities are not historical, but moral and theological. That is, the important discontinuities between Scripture and our contemporary settings are more likely found within us, specifically in our inability and unwillingness to provide and embody wise readings of the texts, than in gaps of historical time. It appears that moral discontinuities also beset Christians in the first century. Whether then or now, greater historical knowledge is not likely to help us overcome these problems. As Lash has suggested:

> To acknowledge that the criteria of fidelity are hard to establish and are frequently problematic is to admit that there is, indeed, a hermeneutical 'gap'. But this 'gap' does not lie, in the last resort, between what was once 'meant' and what might be 'meant' today. It lies, rather, between what was once achieved, intended, or 'shown', and what might be achieved, intended, or 'shown' today. The poles of Christian interpretation are, on the one hand, 'the testimony of Jesus' in his own time and in the time of those who first sought to share that testimony and, on the other hand, such continued sharing in that testimony as may be demanded of us today.[7]

That is why we need to engage in both readings of the texts and readings of the world. As a part of that engagement, we will need to explore the implications of the historical discontinuities between Scripture and contemporary social contexts. As we argued in Chapter 2, we will need to develop and deploy critical virtues for such explorations. At the same time, however, we need to remember that those historical discontinuities should not determine our strategies for faithful reading and faithful living in the present.

Rather, our aim should be to overcome the moral discontinuities between Scripture and us. We only overcome these by becoming people of character formed and transformed by the Holy Spirit. Wise interpretation of Scripture both requires and occasions the virtues of Christian discipleship embodied in and through particular Christian communities. As Richard Hays has argued in relation to Paul's letters (specifically 2 Corinthians 3):

> In the new covenant according to Paul, true reading both presupposes and produces the transformation of readers. Only readers made competent by the Spirit can throw back the veil and perceive the sense of Scripture; those who have not turned to the Lord who is Spirit are necessarily trapped in the script, with minds hardened and veiled. At the same time, readers who do by the aid of the Spirit discover the glory of God in Scripture are necessarily transformed by the experience.[8]

Or, in Nicholas Lash's suggestive image, the social embodiment of Christian life necessary for interpreting Scripture entails 'performing the Scriptures' under the guidance of the Holy Spirit.[9]

Our interpretation of Scripture – and our willingness to have our lives interpreted *by* Scripture – have as their goal a performance of Scripture. As we indicated earlier, scriptural interpretation requires social embodiment. Lash puts it as follows:

> Christian practice, as interpretative action, consists in the *performance* of texts which are construed as 'rendering', bearing witness to, one whose words and deeds, discourse and suffering, 'rendered' the truth of God in human history. The performance of the New Testament enacts the conviction that these texts are most appropriately read as the story of Jesus, the story of everyone else, and the story of God.[10]

Lash's image illumines the practice of interpreting Scripture in and through Christian communities by pointing to the importance of not simply reading the Scriptures, but of actually performing them. Such performances require the development of well-formed character.

Our performances of Scripture vary both in breadth and in depth. Newly baptized members of the community will likely have a narrower range of options and a more superficial grasp of the texts; they may lack the requisite skills and virtues necessary for masterful performance. Such skills and virtues are important, we have suggested, because they enable Christian communities to 'think in common' under the guidance of the Holy Spirit about how to relate the biblical texts to the particular material realities, cultural conditions, and concrete situations in which we find ourselves.

In order to learn to become excellent performers of Scripture, newly initiated members will need to be guided by others in Christian communities whose skills and virtues are more varied, developed, and habituated. Such exemplars guide the newly initiated, in their teaching and in their lives, in showing how to make the links between discernment and performance of the texts.[11]

Pre-eminently, however, the paradigm for those who can guide newly initiated members in Christian life will be those who are in the 'perfected communion of saints'. The performances of the saints are paradigmatic because they represent the greatest range and depth of the skills and virtues of praxis, the most complete representations of the hermeneutical virtue of practical wisdom. On this point, Athanasius's comments are as eloquent as they are instructive:

> For the searching and right understanding of the Scriptures there is need of a good life and a pure soul, and for Christian virtue to guide the mind to grasp, so far as human nature can, the truth concerning God the Word. One cannot possibly understand the teaching of the saints unless one has a pure mind and is trying to imitate their life. Anyone who wants to look at sunlight naturally wipes his eye clear first, in order to make at any rate some approximation to the purity of that on which he looks; and a person wishing to see a city or country goes to the place in order to do so. Similarly, anyone who wishes to understand the mind of the sacred writers must first cleanse his own life, and approach the saints by copying their deeds.[12]

Though Athanasius is unduly concerned with understanding the 'mind' of the sacred writers, his primary point is important. In the performances of the lives of the saints, believers encounter diverse ways of living faithfully before God. As Kenneth Surin describes it:

> [T]he perfected *communio sanctorum* has a crucial regulative role to play in the process of helping all Christians to acquire the requisite skills for understanding the textual world created by the biblical narrative. The saints are the true interpreters of Scripture.[13]

Moreover, the saints are paradigms for Christian life, both personally and corporately, not because of who they are in themselves, but because of the Triune God to whom the pattern of their lives witness.

Ultimately, we read and perform Scripture in the hope that our own lives will be transformed into the likeness of Christ. Such transformation takes place in and through the formation of communities of disciples. That is, the likeness of Christ is manifest not simply in isolated individuals, but in the life of believing communities. Such communities of committed disciples are both the presupposition and the goal of interpreting Scripture. As Hays has argued in relation to Paul's readings of Scripture (our Old Testament):

> No reading of Scripture can be legitimate, then, if it fails to shape the readers into a community that embodies the love of God as shown forth in Christ. This criterion slashes away all frivolous or self-serving readings, all readings that aggrandize the interpreter, all merely clever readings. True interpretation of Scripture leads us into unqualified giving of our lives in service within the community whose vocation is to reenact the obedience of the Son of God who loved us and gave himself for us. Community in the likeness of Christ is cruciform; therefore right interpretation must be cruciform.[14]

In order for our interpretation and our lives to be cruciform, we need to learn to become people of character. That entails our learning to read and perform the Scriptures 'in communion' with other disciples, both the saints and the saints-in-the-making.

Unfortunately, however, this need points to one of the more problematic aspects of our perspective. For while we *need* to read Scripture in and through the practices of Christian communities, there is a distressing paucity of vital Christian communities in the contemporary contexts of North America and Great Britain. Such common life as we do experience is often impoverished.

To be sure, there are some communities that are doing a remarkable job of socializing their members. Unfortunately, the character of the people socialized in these contexts often reflects corrupted conceptions of Christian life instead of wise readings and performances of Scripture. That is a further reason why we think the most important discontinuities between Scripture and our world are not historical, but instead moral and theological, reflecting our failure to become people of the Holy Spirit who perform the Scriptures in our lives.

We need to recover those contexts in which we learn to become Christians with well-formed character if we are going to understand adequately and perform the Scriptures for Christian ethics. That is, we need to recover a common life among disciples of Jesus Christ. By that we do not simply want to point to ecumenical conversations and agreements, though overcoming ecclesial divisions is an important task for the witness of the

Church's unity. But, more generally, we want to point towards the recovery of Christian communities, some of which will be ecclesially specified and others which will not, in which people's characters can be formed into the likeness of Christ.

## THE PATHOS OF CHRISTIAN COMMUNITIES

In one of Peter de Vries's novels, *Comfort Me With Apples*, the main character is a man named Chick Swallow. Swallow is appalled by the spiritual banality of middle-class life. While he is himself preoccupied with style and an aesthetic life, Swallow also is a penetrating critic of conventional religion and the sentimentality it inspires. As Swallow watches worshippers hurrying towards church, he gives complacent thanks: 'There, but for the grace of God, go I.'[15]

That feeling seems to be shared by many people in our culture. Too many people who are looking for the grace of God fear that by identifying with a local church they are more likely to find a shallow piety than the life-giving Spirit. Looking for the bread of life, they find little more than an occasional pot-luck supper. People who are searching for a genuine community of friendship discover (at best) little more than an enclave of superficial friendliness. The very notion of Christians gathering together, which in social settings other than our own has often constituted a political (and often subversive) act, in our context often seems to be little more than a way of calling another meeting to order.

Angela Tilby has described this sense that Christian communities are either absent or too impoverished to matter with particular power. She writes:

> I am disturbed to discover that the playwright Dennis Potter who has through this decade been intensely aware of the pain and ambiguity of our condition feels he *cannot* enter the community of formal Christian believing because he believes the jollity, the triviality and the half-truths masking suffering would deprive him of his power to write.[16]

It is a judgement on the Church when we allow our gatherings to become mere reflections of the culture rather than communities whose readings and performances testify to the crucified and risen

Christ. Indeed, the paucity of vital Christian communities is at least in part the result of a bifurcation of our social world where the basic options are individualism and collectivism.

This point has been made by Alasdair MacIntyre in *After Virtue*.[17] MacIntyre argues that every culture has within it a stock of 'characters', types that furnish people with a cultural and moral ideal and that morally legitimate a mode of social existence. MacIntyre argues that in modern Western societies there are three such 'characters', namely the Rich Aesthete, the Manager and the Therapist. The Manager represents the collectivist realm of bureaucratic rationality, whereas the Rich Aesthete and the Therapist represent the individualist realm of private feelings and values. As MacIntyre argues:

> The bifurcation of the contemporary social world into a realm of the organizational in which ends are taken to be given and are not available for rational scrutiny and a realm of the personal in which judgment and debate about values are central factors, but in which no rational social resolution of issues is available, finds its internalization, its inner representation in the relation of the individual self to the roles and *characters* of social life.[18]

According to MacIntyre, we typically see ourselves in terms of two modes of social life: one in which the free choices of isolated individuals is sovereign, and one in which the bureaucracy is sovereign precisely so that it may limit the free choices of isolated individuals.[19]

A similar analysis is provided by Martin Buber. Buber notes that 'individualism sees man only in relation to himself, but collectivism does not see *man* at all, it sees only "society". With the former, man's face is distorted, with the latter it is masked.'[20] Buber argues that in either case, the human person (who exists, as person, only in relationship) is eclipsed. Hence Buber speaks of the need 'to smash the false alternative with which the thought of our epoch is shot through – that of "individualism" or "collectivism"'.[21] Indeed, Buber goes so far as to suggest that the lack of community that he sees as characteristic of modern societies has rendered authentic prayer virtually impossible.[22]

We contend that in such social contexts there may be Christian 'communities' that exist in a minimalist sense (i.e. people who gather together and understand themselves in one way or another as 'Christians'). But they often do so at the price of failing to embody an alternative to the destructive forces of individualism and collectivism. Indeed, in our societies such 'communities' are often better described, in a term used by Robert Bellah and his colleagues, as 'lifestyle enclaves'. These are places where people go (often, in MacIntyre's terms, for 'aesthetic' or 'therapeutic' reasons) to find people like themselves, but lacking the virtues of authentic Christian community.[23]

An important consideration for our readings of the world is the fact that, at least in the contexts of modern Western societies, Christian communities that are reading and performing Scripture for the sake of faithful witness to the world are impoverished. Consequently, we need to work towards eliminating the moral discontinuities between Scripture and our own social settings. In short, we need to work towards recovering a common life through engaging in particular friendships, practices, skills and habits learned through study of Scripture and the traditions of the Church.

Such communities will need to be in but not of the world. That is a difficult task, for we need to foster communities that are sufficiently distinct from the world to enable the formation and transformation of Christian character yet also involved in witness and ministries in the world. In what follows we provide a sketch of some practices of the Christian communities that we want to recover.

## REHABILITATING CHRISTIAN COMMUNITIES

In the last chapter we briefly mentioned the usage of the notion of 'world' in the letter of James. We want to return to that letter, and to a particular passage in that letter, to suggest why the task of becoming disciples in Christian communities involves turning from the 'world' to God. The passage revolves around James 4.4: 'Unfaithful creatures! Do you not know that friendship with the world is enmity with God? Therefore whoever wishes to be a friend of the world makes himself an enemy of God.'[24] This is not a pleasant statement to ponder, yet it points to some key themes in understanding Christian life and the vocation of Christian communities.

The section of the letter that begins at 3.13 and concludes at

4.10 is marked by sharp contrasts, contrasts whereby we are urged to replace one way of life with another. Corresponding to these contrasts is another that divides two measures of reality, derived from different sources and leading to different actions.

The problem with the first measure of reality, here identified as 'the world', is that it is characterized by bitter jealousy, selfish ambition, disorder and covetousness; it does not come from above, but is earthly, unspiritual, devilish. The 'world' is not the place of trees and cities, football and one's work; the 'world' is, as Luke T. Johnson puts it, 'a system of untrameled [sic] desire and arrogance'.[25]

In direct contrast, James describes an alternative measure of reality. That reality is marked by a wisdom which comes 'from above', a wisdom which is peaceable, gentle, open to reason, full of mercy and good fruits. It derives from the spirit which God made to dwell in us. The contrast between the 'world' and God is not some sort of cosmic or metaphysical dualism in which matter is denigrated. Rather, it is an ethical dualism characterized by a choice between living in friendship with a 'world' of envy and ambition, and living in friendship with the God from whom all wisdom and peace and righteousness flow.

James, like Paul in Rom. 6, urges his readers to shift allegiance from one power to the other, from one realm of reality to the other. A 'turning' is required, a reorientation of one's entire existence towards God and away from that which separates and divides through jealousy and ambition. The importance of this reorientation can be seen by an examination of James's use of the language of friendship.

While in modern societies friendship often means a kind of well-wishing collegiality or a superficial affection for another person, in ancient societies friendship designated much more. For example, according to Aristotle in the *Nicomachean Ethics*, friendship is at the very heart of the moral life; in and through friendship we become certain kinds of people rather than other kinds.

So to be a friend of the 'world', a 'world' that James understands as marked by the exclusion of God and a realm of untrammelled desire and arrogance, is to become marked by that same desire and arrogance and thus to be at enmity with God. To be a friend of the 'world' is to see things the way the 'world' does, to define my identity on the 'world's terms. And that, so James suggests, is to see things wrongly and to be caught in the grips of devilish unfaithfulness.

More particularly, James suggests that we see things wrongly when we have friendship with the 'world' because the 'world' revolves around envy. Envy causes moral blindness, an inability to see things and other people clearly and compassionately. Envy is caused by my identifying who I am with what I have. So I must have more and more, creating an insatiable greed and a correlative insecurity. If another person has more, then that person is a threat and makes me less of a person. What fuels envy is competitiveness, the desire to measure my worth by an analysis of what I have compared to everyone else.

This attempt to 'keep up with the Joneses' is prevalent in our societies. It reflects an often desperate attempt to climb the ladder of success and recognition so that 'I' will be admired and respected. According to James, such activity leads to social unrest, divisiveness, hostility, and even murder. For when living by such a measure, I can only be more if I eliminate and/or marginalize the other.

Our attempt to live in friendship with the 'world' undermines the vitality of Christian communities. And, in modern Western societies, we are left with a bifurcated realm where the choices are individualism and collectivism. If we are to become faithful disciples, we need to reject the standards of the 'world' and reorient our life towards God. This points to the need for developing those 'hidden spaces' referred to in our discussion of Isaiah 49.[26]

In the same way that James suggests the desire to be a friend of the world puts a person at enmity with God, so he suggests that the alternative is to draw near to God in friendship. Abraham is designated by James as a 'friend of God' because of his faithfulness before God (Jas. 2.23). Likewise, we need to become friends of God by responding to God with lives of faithful discipleship.[27]

But, it might be objected, all of this sounds a little harsh. Why can't we be friends both with the 'world' and with God? James's call to conversion is addressed to such 'double-minded' people (Jas. 4.8). Being double-minded is characteristic of those people who want to live in friendship with both the 'world' and God. But, James suggests, you cannot do so; for the attempt to do so means that you hedge your bets and ultimately are still blinded by the 'world's' standards of envy, jealousy and ambition.

Because so many of us – then and now – want to live double-minded lives, the structure of James's letter as a whole, and in particular 3.13–4.10, is a reminder that the process of turning from the 'world' to God is never over. It must be continually renewed. The reconstruction of our lives is an ongoing process that requires us to become part of communities that enable us continually to cleanse our hands, purify our hearts, and draw near to God (Jas. 4.8). As Luke T. Johnson puts it in reference to the addressees of James's letter, 'Although that word which shapes their Christian identity has been "implanted" in them, they must still "accept it with meekness", they must continually become "doers" of it; therefore, even for those already converted, the prophetic call to conversion is appropriate.'[28]

Contrary to those in the Christian tradition who have denigrated James because the letter appears to suggest that we are justified by works rather than faith, James's understanding of faith and works is not opposed to the notion that we are justified by grace through faith. Rather, James is emphasizing that the vocation of Christian discipleship is an integral part of the grace with which God befriends us, and that the process of learning to turn away from friendship with the 'world' and learning to become friends of God is a process that takes time. We have to unlearn the standards of the world, refuse the temptations to become 'double-minded' people, and learn to become faithful disciples of Jesus Christ.

This passage in James suggests the task of becoming disciples requires us to recover the centrality of Christian communities for our readings and performances of Scripture. Too often we associate Christian life in general, and reading Scripture in particular, with an individualistic 'me and Jesus' way of life. In such a view, religion is seen as something you or I privately experience, which we then may or may not share with others.[29]

But Christian discipleship is anything but individualistic. Becoming a Christian involves being incorporated into particular communities of disciples set on the journey of becoming friends of God and bearing witness to the good news of God's inbreaking Kingdom. Baptism, specifically baptism into Christ, through the Triune name is the ritual activity that signifies our transition from friendship with the 'world' into friendship with God. Baptism signifies our incorporation into the eschatological reign of God, and we learn to participate in God's reign through participation in

Christian communities. Thus baptism is at once a sacramental act of the Church *and* an ongoing process of 'living into your baptism' through lives of discipleship in friendship with God.

In and through our participation in Christian communities – called into being and sustained by the Triune God and marked as the Body of Christ – we are enabled to engage in the process of unlearning the ways of the 'world' and learning how to pattern our lives in Jesus Christ. We must refuse to allow the standards of the 'world' to define our lives and our communities. Patterning our lives in Christ closely links baptism and our readings and performances of Scripture. Baptism inserts us into the realm of disciples-in-the-making who read, and are read by, Scripture, so that we might live more faithfully before God.

Thus one way in which we can work towards recovering vital Christian communities is by recovering their distinctiveness in opposition to the destructive tendencies of the 'world'. Christian life involves a turning from friendship with the 'world' to friendship with God. However, such a characterization in and of itself is inadequate. For it too easily can be assumed that Christian life involves some kind of flight from the profane world into the realm of a safe and secure sacred haven. Christian life, a life patterned in Jesus Christ, can never be a flight from the world which is an arena of social, economic, and political interactions, conflicts, and cooperative endeavours. Christians must be willing to engage such a world.

Thus there is a second way in which we ought to work towards recovering Christian communities, and that is by practising hospitality. This hospitality should be modelled on the fellowship required for the right practice of the Eucharist (cf. 1 Cor. 11.17ff.).

Further, such hospitality should lead us to become people who welcome strangers into our midst. This is because the Eucharist, like baptism, has a twofold character. It is a sacramental act of the Church in which people participate in praise and thanksgiving. It is also an ongoing practice of eucharistic living. The practice of the eucharist both sustains Christian community and calls for hospitality to others. Eucharistic living is thus closely linked to reading and performing Scripture. We need to read Scripture 'in communion' with fellow believers, and we need also to be ready to welcome those who for one reason or another are outside that communion.[30]

In order to understand what eucharistic hospitality might mean, consider two pictures. In the first one, a person is the secretary of a rather large United Methodist church in a small town in North Carolina. Not much happens from day to day in the office of this church: the phones have to be answered, the bulletins run off, materials sent out for the various meetings of the church. Every now and then, however, someone drops in looking for some food, bus fare, or some other kind of assistance. The people of the church have set up a kitchen in order to feed the poor, and they have a fund available for assisting the poor in emergencies. Yet when someone comes making such requests, the secretary employs two basic tests before giving out any food or money. First, the secretary gives only to people who are temporarily down on their luck, but who are otherwise respectable and upstanding members of the community. Second, the secretary does not give anything to strangers, for there is no way of knowing about the strangers' character or their motives.

In the second picture, a young woman is out hunting with her husband in the Colorado wilderness. She is a wildlife biologist, he is a wildlife technician. They separate for a few minutes late in the afternoon. The woman realizes it is getting late, and she is on an area of the mountain unfamiliar to her. She begins to follow a stream but, as she does, she only gets more lost. As it gets dark, she fires out her warning shots. There is no response. It is cold outside, and she knows she may be in trouble. The darkness falls, and she is still wandering around lost. Finally, through the trees she sees some lights in a secluded cabin. She has no idea what might happen to her if she knocks on the door, and she is very anxious. Hesitantly she goes up to the door, and she knocks gently. A person opens the door, and the woman says urgently, 'Please help me – I'm lost.' The people in the house comfort her and tell her, 'It's OK. You're safe. We'll take care of you. We are Christians here.'

Both stories are true. Yet if we were asked which story more accurately characterizes life in contemporary societies, we would have a hard time answering. On the one hand, something within us joins the secretary in our fear of strangers. Confronting any stranger is a disorienting experience, for it renders us vulnerable and uncertain as to how to respond. And in our societies in particular, we have all – especially ministers and employees of churches – encountered or heard about con artists knocking on the doors of churches, complete with phoney stories of suffering and need. It does not take many such stories to make us somewhat callous to the requests of strangers.

And yet for Christians there is something else within us that tells us that we ought to be willing to take the risk. We admire the people who showed hospitality to the lost hunter and reassured her that 'we are Christians here'. We remember the passage in Hebrews 13.2, 'Do not neglect to show hospitality to strangers, for thereby some have entertained angels unawares.' We are afraid to confront strangers, and yet we know that doing so is integral to Christian life. We know that we should show hospitality to the stranger, but how? What would it mean – or perhaps what would it take – for disciples of Jesus Christ to be prepared to say, 'It's O K. You're safe. We'll take care of you. We are Christians here'?

In short, we need particular Christian communities composed of disciples who embody distinctive practices and virtues of relating to one another as well as to strangers.[31] We need communities whose particular identity of bearing witness to God's Kingdom is reflected in an openness to others. If we are to be able to understand who strangers are and what they might need in the way of hospitality, then we need to recover a sense of what it means to say 'we are Christians here'.

More precisely, the real issue is not an 'if-then' proposition. It is not a matter of first recovering a distinctive sense of the eschatological context of Christian community and subsequently asking about strangers, their needs and the question of hospitality. Rather, as the New Testament makes abundantly clear, we discover and recover Christian community *precisely in* being a Eucharistic people who, modelling their life on the fellowship of the Eucharist, show hospitality to strangers. Only by being the kind of people open to receiving strangers as friends of God do we discover what it means to be a community bearing witness to the openness and graciousness of God's inbreaking Kingdom. By welcoming strangers into our midst, we are transformed and welcomed into a new life.

As John Koenig has suggested, it is no accident that the three major festivals of the Church – Christmas, Easter and Pentecost – all have to do with the advent of a divine stranger.[32] In each case the newcomer offers blessings that are difficult to comprehend.

The child in the manger, the traveller on the road to Emmaus, and the mighty wind of the Spirit all meet us as mysterious visitors. They interrupt our everyday lives, and in that interruption they enable us to see things differently.

Such interruptions and challenges to our everyday notions of strangers and friends, insiders and outsiders, characterize Jesus' ministry. Jesus refuses to allow people to be excluded or marginalized because they are no longer 'pure' or 'clean' by the standards of insiders. For example, in Luke 7.34 Jesus describes his own activity as follows: 'The Son of man has come eating and drinking; and you say, "Behold, a glutton and a drunkard, a friend of tax collectors and sinners!"' The term 'friend of tax collectors and sinners' was meant as a contemptuous, derogatory reference; Jesus is not playing by the rules of 'respectable' society. Jesus befriends people wherever he encounters them, and in particular he befriends those excluded and marginalized by 'established' society and the 'conventional' powers: the poor, the sick, the outcast.

The community established by Jesus' table fellowship offers people a welcoming place where they are honoured guests. There people are recognized and treated as God's children regardless of their prior life or the circumstances into which they were born. Moreover, Jesus' first (and later!) disciples came from all walks of life and from a diversity of backgrounds, some of which were suspect; it was no small thing for them to be ready to receive one another as friends. But by enjoying table fellowship with particular people, Jesus transforms those who had otherwise been isolated and alienated from one another into a community united by his friendship (See Mk.2.15ff; Lk.19.1ff.).

The strangers Jesus welcomes into his community are not always the unknown or the different. They often are people we know, but who are alienated from us in one way or another. So Jesus welcomes Zacchaeus. He also urges the 'insiders' to seek out the exiles and those who are marginalized and bring them back into the community. We are to seek out the lost sheep, find the lost coin, welcome back the lost son. When the lost son 'comes to himself' – in important ways he is a stranger even to himself – he returns home repentant to a father who is running out to meet him. The son discovers that in God's world repentance and forgiveness are more like a homecoming banquet than like sackcloth and ashes. For Jesus, Christian community is bound up with a willingness to welcome the stranger – whomever she or he might be – as a friend and honoured guest at the banquet.

Through his ministry, and particularly through his table fellowship, Jesus breaks down the walls of separation and hostility and creates a new and open community marked by unity and peace. That transformation culminates in the cross and resurrection, where all that separates us from one another and from God – all that which prevents us from being hospitable communities – has been overcome.

Thus the renewed community centred on the life, death and resurrection of Jesus Christ has as particular focal points the recollection of Jesus' table-fellowship and his crucifixion and resurrection. Perhaps especially in our day we are likely to discover Christian community, and thereby gain a renewed sense of the significance of strangers, to the extent that we remember we are not only a Baptismal people, but a Eucharistic people also.

We have suggested that the rehabilitation of Christian communities involves both turning from the world to God and welcoming strangers through Eucharistic hospitality. While turning from the world to God might connote a flight from everyday reality into some secure haven, the vocation of providing hospitality to strangers requires an openness to others. But while both of these themes are crucial for understanding how Christian communities should be related to the wider culture, they are still incomplete.

They still seem to suggest that Christian communities *must* exist apart from the rest of society. That Christian communities *can* do so should be accepted without question. There is a powerful witness to be discovered in serious and intentional Christian communities whose separate existence represents a stark contrast to the 'ways of the world'. Moreover, that some Christian communities *should* do so should also be accepted; all Christians should be thankful that there are monastic communities whose separate existence enables them continually to pray to God for the sake of our salvation and the redemption of the world. One way of serving the world is to live apart from it so that, on the one hand, those who do not know God can see what it means to live in friendship with God; and, on the other hand, all of God's creation can be lifted up in prayer before God in the hope that the Kingdom of God will soon come in its fullness.

At the same time, however, we need to recognize that for many – indeed most – Christians, a significant part of our lives is spent living and working in the wider society. Thus a third context for recovering the centrality of Christian communities is by reclaiming the mission to serve in the world. And the crucial question here is: if we are going to live and work in the wider society, how should we do so?

One might answer this question by claiming that we must adapt ourselves to the wider society. There is the Kingdom of God, represented by the Church, and when we are in that sphere we are expected to live by its standards and commitments. But there are also the Kingdoms of this world and when we are in those spheres we are expected to live by their standards and commitments.

In such a view questions are never asked about whether or not a Christian ought to serve in the military, or become a politician, or a lawyer, or an entertainer. Because we can't expect to 'change the world', and because, after all, discipleship really applies only to the sphere of the Kingdom of God, we should simply decide what we ought to do and then adapt ourselves to the standards we find there.

This picture, popular among many people, needs to be discarded as a misleading and distorting image of the vocation of Christian communities and Christian life. It is misleading and distorting for several reasons. First, such a view represents the attempt to live as the 'double-minded' people whom James (4.8) indicts because their double-mindedness means they ultimately are going to live by the world's standards and its measure, rather than God's.

Second, and closely related to James's indictment, such a picture of Christian communities and the 'world' is predicated on a misleading understanding of the kind of creatures we are. We are not people who can live schizophrenic lives without cost to our identities. We are not people for whom the decisions we make and the actions we take have no bearing on who we are and what we become. We develop particular habits through our decisions and actions, and those habits shape our personal identities. If we are deciding and acting by the world's standards rather than by God's, then we are likely to become and remain people of the world rather than people of God.

Third, such a picture represents a spiritualization of discipleship and of the Church's vocation, so that Christian life is primarily – if not exclusively – about private religious experiences and emotions, having little if anything to do with the structures and attitudes of 'the real world'. Anybody who understands Christian life and Christian ethics in scriptural terms should not tolerate such a watering down of the mission of Christian communities. Jesus was not in the business of simply bolstering people's self-esteem or helping people to have 'peak experiences'. Rather, he was in the business of proclaiming the Kingdom of God in both word and deed. That involved transforming people's lives and restoring them to wholeness, to be sure. But more fundamentally, the message of the Kingdom challenged those structures and powers in the world that are destructive of human life and of human relationships.

When Jesus sends out his disciples, he does so in order that we will proclaim the gospel in word and deed. And he does so in order that people everywhere might know the good news of God's forgiving, reconciling grace. When we find Jesus telling Nicodemus that he must be 'born anew' (John 3.3), when we find Paul writing that anyone who is in Christ is a 'new creation' (2 Cor. 5.17), when we find Paul suggesting that by being baptized we have now 'put on Christ' (Gal. 3.27), we are being reminded that Christian discipleship involves the formation of a new identity shaped in response to God's gracious initiative.

Because of that new identity, and the importance of not living a double-minded life, we need to ask questions about what kinds of lives Christians ought (and perhaps ought not) to lead. Such questions are important, for we need to remember that when we serve and work in particular social settings we are to do so *as followers of Jesus Christ*. As Jesus prays in his high priestly prayer, 'They do not belong to the world, just as I do not belong to the world. Sanctify them in the truth; your word is truth. As you have sent me into the world, so I have sent them into the world. And for their sakes I sanctify myself, so that they also may be sanctified in truth' (John 17.16–19 NRSV). We are the ones sent into the world by Jesus, and we are sent to be witnesses to the gracious Truth who is God.

We need to remember that our witness is most powerful and most authentic when we witness to the good news through the lives we lead.[33] The saints of the Church are those people whose lives speak most eloquently of the gospel of Jesus Christ. Their lives are paradigmatic examples for us, enabling us to judge a little more wisely what we should do and how we should live if we are to be faithful disciples of Jesus Christ.

And those lives, if they truly represent lives patterned in Jesus Christ, are bound to strike us as being a little strange. They are people who seem to see and do things differently. They are the kind of people who serve rather than dominate, who forgive and seek reconciliation rather than bear grudges and persist in alienating others, who feed the hungry and visit those in prison without any fanfare or expectations of return. They are the kind of people who speak out against injustice, who are more concerned about others' welfare than their own, the kind of people willing to risk their lives so that others may live. They reflect in their lives something of the glory of God revealed in Jesus Christ, and because they do they are bound to seem rather strange to us.

These people often remain nameless and faceless to many of us, principally because they do not try to draw attention to themselves. But even so, their lives speak eloquently to those who encounter them; they represent masterful 'performances' of Scripture in whose presence people are enabled to see more clearly what they should do and how they should live.

But there are also people whose lives have become more generally known. For example, there is Judge Olivier, an Afrikaner judge in Alan Paton's historically based novel *Ah, But Your Land Is Beautiful*. The story is from the early days of post-Second World War apartheid in South Africa when the emerging laws could still be tested. An Afrikaner judge, responding to the urgent invitation of a black pastor, visits the latter's church on Maundy Thursday to show the parishioners that not all whites have turned against them. Simply by worshipping in this church the judge risks his career. But the pastor, who perhaps knows the judge's integrity better than he himself does, has made a further request – namely, that he join with members of the congregation in a foot-washing service. The feet presented to him are those of a woman who has worked as a servant in his house for more than thirty years. Some of the worshippers gasp as Jan Christiaan Olivier kneels before Martha Fortuin. The story concludes: 'Then he took both her feet in his hands with gentleness, for they were no doubt tired with much serving, and he kissed them both. Then Martha Fortuin and many others in the Holy Church of Zion fell a-weeping.' Novelist Paton adds that this incident was picked up by some of the leading English and American newspapers and that Judge Olivier's career was indeed curtailed.[34]

According to the standards of white South African Society, Judge Olivier is strange. He did the unexpected, in fact he did the unthinkable. His actions in this situation provide a glimpse of the glory of God. There was a cost to his discipleship; by becoming strange to others, he ran the risk of all strangers. He was marginalized by the dominant culture, and his career was curtailed. He suffered because he served. But as disciples of one who challenged the dominant culture and ended up nailed to a cross, should we expect anything different?

In our service in the world we need to be willing to become strange to others. It is the strangeness of a Samaritan stopping by the side of the road to take care of someone in need. It is the strangeness of throwing a banquet rather than setting up a doghouse when a lost child returns. It is the strangeness of being a witness to God's inbreaking Kingdom through faithful discipleship patterned in Jesus Christ.

Or perhaps it is the strangeness of an Armenian woman's response to her suffering. The Armenian Christians are a people who have experienced centuries of suffering and know that their worship is surrounded by a cloud of martyred witnesses. A Turkish officer had raided and looted an Armenian home. He killed the aged parents and gave the daughters to the soldiers, keeping the eldest daughter for himself. Some time later she escaped and trained as a nurse. As time passed, she found herself nursing in a ward of Turkish officers. One night, by the light of a lantern, she saw the face of this officer. He was so gravely ill that without exceptional nursing he would die. The days passed, and he recovered. One day, the doctor stood by the bed with her and said to him, 'But for her devotion to you, you would be dead.' He looked at her and said, 'We have met before, haven't we?'

'Yes,' she said, 'we have met before.' 'Why didn't you kill me?' he asked. She replied, 'I am a follower of him who said "Love your enemies".'[35]

If we are to recover the centrality of Christian communities for Christian life and ethics, we need to learn to live and worship in ways that form people to be able to respond in ways like this Armenian woman. Whether the issue is as concrete and particular as learning to love our enemies or as abstract and general as developing strategies for dealing with world hunger or international debt, Christian communities need to be forming people whose service in the world will be best described as wise performances of Scripture.[36] In order to provide such formation, Christian communities need to turn from the 'world' to God, to practise Eucharistic hospitality by welcoming strangers into our midst, and to enable people to serve in the world.

We began this section by citing Peter De Vries's character's comment on watching people go to church: 'There but for the grace of God, go I.' In so far as people genuinely say that, it is a judgement on the Church. But if we recover the centrality of Christian communities, the vocation of living in a manner patterned in Jesus Christ by performing the Scriptures, then perhaps Christians can escape the judgement implied in that comment. Instead, it will become an affirmation that it is by the grace of God that we are enabled to live in a way that faithfully witnesses to God's Kingdom. As we live and serve, we can say, 'There, by the grace of God, we go.' Only in that way, by producing masterful performances of Scripture, will we be able to have overcome the moral discontinuities between Scripture and our own lives.

## CONCLUSION

In this chapter we have both recognized the many discontinuities between Scripture and contemporary Christian life in the present, and argued that we need to understand these discontinuities in different ways than we normally have done. Such a reorientation consists of two main components. First, we ought not to presume that we start with trying to discover what the text 'meant' and then discuss what it 'means' today. Rather we need to work analogically and dialectically between the past and the present, seeking to find ways of making our performances of Scripture in the present faithful to the God to whom the scriptural texts bear witness.

Secondly, we need to recognize that the determinative discontinuities are more the result of our contemporary failure to embody faithful living in Christian communities than anything ingredient in historical differences. We are called by God to embody faithful living so that the claims made in Scripture and by the Church will be not only intelligible but also persuasive. That entails recovering the friendships and practices of Christian communities in and through which we learn to become people of character able to read and perform Scripture wisely.

However, we need to recognize that even vital Christian communities do not simply reflect harmonious agreement about how Scripture ought to be read and performed. People disagree over how best to understand and perform particular texts, and those disagreements can erupt into serious conflicts over the Church's identity and mission. How should we understand and deal with the existence of interpretive disputes within believing communities? To such issues we now turn.

## NOTES

1. This understanding, so widespread in its usage that it has (unfortunately) become something of a commonplace, was made famous by Krister Stendahl in his article 'Biblical Theology, Contemporary', in *The Interpreter's Dictionary of the Bible, vol. 1* (Nashville, TN: Abingdon, 1962), pp. 418–32. For a critical analysis of Stendahl's argument, see Ben C. Ollenburger, 'What Krister Stendahl "Meant" – A Normative Critique of "Descriptive Biblical Theology"', *Horizons in Biblical Theology* 8 (1986), pp. 61–98.

2. See our discussion in Chapter 1.

3. We owe the metaphor of the relay race to Nicholas Lash, 'What Might Martyrdom Mean?' *Ex Auditu* 1 (1985), p. 16; reproduced in Lash, *Theology on the Way to Emmaus* (London: SCM, 1986), pp. 75–92.

4. Nicholas Lash, 'Interpretation and Imagination', in *Incarnation and Myth: The Debate Continued*, ed. Michael D. Goulder (London: SCM; Grand Rapids, MI: Wm. B. Eerdmans, 1979), pp. 24–5.

5. In 'The Place of Scripture in Christian Ethics', James Gustafson has argued that the primary question in the use of Scripture for moral

analogies is that of control (see *Readings in Moral Theology No. 4: The Use of Scripture in Moral Theology*, eds Charles E. Curran and Richard A. McCormick, SJ (New York: Paulist Press), p. 164). As we argued in Chapter 1, there is no context-independent way to provide control for *any* interpretive practices. Thinking analogically is no more and no less open to abuse than other strategies. Practical wisdom provides the appropriate control.

6. These passages are explicated in greater detail in Stephen E. Fowl, 'Some Uses of Story in Moral Discourse', *Modern Theology* 4 (1988), pp. 293–308; and also *The Story of Christ in the Ethics of Paul* JSNTS 37 (Sheffield, England: JSOT Press, 1990).

7. Lash, 'What Might Martyrdom Mean?', p. 23.

8. Richard Hays, *Echoes of Scripture in the Letters of Paul* (New Haven, CT: Yale University Press, 1989), p. 148.

9. See Nicholas Lash, 'Performing the Scriptures', in *Theology on the Way to Emmaus*, pp. 37–46.

10. ibid., p. 42.

11. For an excellent discussion of the ways in which the early Church understood the importance of exemplars for forming character, see Robert L. Wilken, 'Alexandria: A School for Training in Virtue', in *Schools of Thought in the Christian Tradition*, ed. Patrick Henry (Philadelphia, PA: Fortress, 1984), pp. 15–30.

12. St Athanasius, *The Incarnation of the Word of God* (New York: Macmillan, 1946), p. 96. We are indebted to Stanley Hauerwas, *A Community of Character* (Notre Dame, IN: University of Notre Dame Press, 1981), p. 36, for this quotation.

13. Kenneth Surin, 'The Weight of Weakness', in *The Turnings of Darkness and Light* (Cambridge: Cambridge University Press, 1989), p. 219.

14. Hays, *Echoes of Scripture in the Letters of Paul*, p. 191.

15. Peter De Vries, *Comfort Me With Apples* (Boston: Little, Brown, 1956), p. 35. We are indebted to Ralph Wood's *The Comedy of Redemption* (Notre Dame, IN: University of Notre Dame Press, 1988), esp. pp. 244–6, for this material.

16. Angela Tilby, 'Spirit of the Age', *Christian* 5 (1980), p. 12, cited in Rowan Williams, 'Postmodern Theology and the Judgment of the World', in *Postmodern Theology*, ed. Frederic B. Burnham (New York: Harper & Row, 1989), p. 112.

17. This analysis was first developed in relation to theological discourse in L. Gregory Jones, 'Toward a Recovery of Theological Discourse in United Methodism', *Quarterly Review* 9 (1989), pp. 19–22.

18. MacIntyre, *After Virtue*, 2nd edn (London: Duckworth; Notre Dame, IN: University of Notre Dame Press, 1984), p. 34.

19. See ibid., p. 35.

20. Martin Buber, *Between Man and Man*, tr. Ronald Gregor Smith (London: Kegan Paul, 1927), p. 200. We are indebted to Nicholas Lash's *Easter in Ordinary* (London: SCM; Charlottesville, VA: University Press of Virginia, 1988) for directing us to these passages

in Buber's thought.
21. Buber, *Between Man and Man*, p. 202.
22. See Buber, *A Believing Humanism*, tr. Maurice Friedman (New York: Simon & Schuster, 1967), p. 200.
23. See Robert Bellah *et al.*, *Habits of the Heart* (Berkeley, CA: University of California Press, 1985), pp. 71–5.
24. We are indebted to Luke T. Johnson's fascinating and insightful essay, 'Friendship with the World/Friendship with God: A Study of Discipleship in James', for directing us to this passage and its connection to discipleship and the vocation of Christian communities. The essay is found in *Discipleship in the New Testament*, ed. Fernando F. Segovia (Philadelphia, PA: Fortress, 1985), pp. 166–83.
25. ibid., p. 171.
26. See our discussion in Chapter 2.
27. For contemporary discussions of the importance of friendship with God, see Paul Wadell, *Friendship and the Moral Life* (Notre Dame, IN: University of Notre Dame Press, 1989); L. Gregory Jones, *Transformed Judgment*.
28. Johnson, 'Friendship with the World/Friendship with God', p. 177.
29. See Chapter 1 for a discussion of how this emphasis on isolated individuals has infected our conceptions of ethics and interpretation.
30. As we will show in Chapter 5, outsiders have important voices which Christians need to hear as we seek to read and perform the Scriptures wisely.
31. We discuss the interpretive significance of strangers and other outsiders in Chapter 5.
32. John Koenig, *New Testament Hospitality* (Philadelphia, PA: Fortress, 1985), p. 5.
33. James Wm. McClendon has made this point with reference to the importance of biography for theology. See his *Biography as Theology* (Nashville, TN: Abingdon, 1974), recently republished with a new preface (Philadelphia, PA: Trinity Press International, 1990).
34. Alan Paton, *Ah, But Your Land Is Beautiful* (New York: Charles Scribner's Sons, 1981), p. 235, cited in Koenig, *New Testament Hospitality*, p. 61.
35. The story is cited in Geoffrey Wainwright, *Doxology* (London: Epworth; New York: Oxford University Press, 1980), p. 434.
36. Christian communities, in turn, need to be so constituted that they can listen to the concerns and struggles of people who serve in the world. Such communities need to become the sort of communities capable of bearing people's primary allegiance. In this way, Christian community becomes the focus for *both* our readings of the texts and our readings of the world.

# 4

## Being Able to Hear the Word of God: Character-izing Interpretive Disputes

In previous chapters we have argued that issues of character ought to be central to an adequate account of Christian ethics. Further, much of what we have said so far on this issue has tried to undermine the notion that character is simply a component of ethics, something that is optional to be picked up and put down as needed. If our character informs and is informed by all aspects of our actions, thoughts and associations, then we should expect that our character will interact in similar ways with our interpretive practices.

It would be odd, then, if we did not discuss some of the relationships between character and biblical interpretation, particularly in regard to interpretive disputes within Christian communities. If well-formed character is crucial to Christians' ability to live faithfully in the various contexts in which they find themselves, we should also expect that well-formed character will also influence Christians' ability to read, speak and perform the word of the Lord. Having argued this point, we will then examine some of the particular interrelations between character and interpretation as these are presented in situations of interpretive disagreement.

The claim that character and interpretive practices of reading Scripture are intimately related runs counter to the presumptions and practices of modern biblical criticism. Within the academy and the professional societies, scholars form, explicate and execute their interpretive interests so that any competent fellow scholar can evaluate another's interpretive practice regardless of either scholar's character.[1] What one does in one's study or in a conference room need not have any direct bearing on the way one lives one's life. The character of any particular scholar is generally irrelevant to that scholar's professional activities.

The situation should be (but is not always) different for Christian communities. This is because the continuing life of the people of God is intimately tied to their interpretive practice. Unless Christians embody their interpretation of Scripture (thus producing a certain character), their interpretation is in vain. Further, the production and presence of a particular character serves to validate a Christian community's interpretation of Scripture in ways that are simply unacceptable in the modern liberal university's discipline of biblical studies.

Consider this brief example: The basic ecclesial communities of Latin America are among the liveliest and most encouraging manifestations of Christian community today. At the root of their renewed common life is their recovery of Scripture as their book, a book of the people. Within these communities people are reading and interpreting Scripture in ways that enliven their faith and encourage and guide faithful living. Often these interpretations would not count as acceptable readings in the context of a scholarly conference. In these contexts, however, what does count is the manner of life, the character, the practice that issues from these readings. These considerations, more than any others, shape those communities' judgements about what counts as an acceptable reading.[2]

Having made this general point, we should add some qualifications. First, it is false to think that those with well-formed character will always interpret faithfully. Our claim is not that appeals to character are decisive in adjudicating interpretive disputes. Indeed there may be times when judgements about people's character do not become clear until long after the interpretive dispute has either been settled or is no longer relevant. Even so, while judgements about character are always revisable, our claim is that the character of interpreters and Scriptural interpretation are bound up with one another.[3]

Second, it is also false to think that *only* those Christians with well-formed character will be able to interpret and perform the Scriptures faithfully. Very few, if any, people enter the community of disciples with well-formed character. Rather, we begin our struggle to become faithful interpreters and performers of Scripture as incomplete characters. We are often unsure about how to proceed. Sometimes we bear the residue of our past. We are not blank slates simply waiting for the Holy Spirit to transform us into the image of Christ overnight. We should remember that the formation of our character and the relationship of that formation to our interpretive practices is an ongoing process that ultimately awaits completion at 'the day of Jesus Christ' (Phil. 1.6).

On the other hand, it would be a mistake to wait until 'the day of Jesus Christ' to engage in interpretation or to witness to the gospel. Part of the way in which a Christian's character is formed is through the practice of witness and by engaging in conversation with others.

Given these qualifications, our central point remains: Faithful interpretation and performance of Scripture are not simply factors of having the most refined and sophisticated reading strategy. Our character also plays a central role in our ability to interpret and perform Scripture faithfully. It would, however, be impossible to specify in detail how character and interpretation will be interrelated in any particular context. Rather, our aim in this chapter is to examine some interpretive disputes within communities to reflect on the ways character impinges upon interpretive practice and what these reflections imply for people seeking to read in communion.

## PAUL AND THE GALATIANS

Christianity started as a reform movement within Judaism. Thus one of the most pressing questions the earliest Christians had to address concerned the increasing numbers of Gentiles joining their numbers. Did these Gentile followers of the resurrected Christ have to become Jews? That is, did they need to be circumcised and follow the prescriptions of the Torah as any other Jew would? Answers to this question would naturally involve interpretations both of the Church's Scriptures (i.e. the Old Testament in Greek), and of the traditions about the life, death and resurrection of Christ that formed these communities. These interpretations would arise out of the contexts and experiences of the various communities.

Paul, in the epistle to the Galatians, provides one answer to this vexing question.[4] The tenor of the whole epistle makes it clear that Paul is engaged in an interpretive conflict with those who think that faithful Christian living demands that all believers also submit to the Jewish law. Paul holds the opposite view, arguing that the death and resurrection of Christ has established the Church as the renewed Israel of God, in which Gentiles are freely admitted without having to submit to the law. By briefly looking at the argument of Galatians, we can see that Paul offers an interpretation of the life, death and resurrection of Christ and of the activity of God related in the Old Testament to support his argument. His position, however, also rests on his own character and the character he assumes the Galatians to have.

In fact, Paul does not begin his argument by directly entering the interpretive dispute. Rather, he starts with an account of his character and authority as an apostle. He does this by recounting his biography. Paul's point in relating his past life here is to confirm his character as a faithful and true interpreter and performer of the gospel.[5]

Paul is one of those people who enters the community of disciples with a character previously formed by a strong allegiance to another tradition. As he notes, 'You have heard about my former life in Judaism, how I persecuted the church of God violently and tried to destroy it. I advanced in Judaism beyond many of my own age among my own people, so extremely zealous was I for the traditions of my fathers' (1.13–14).

As is well known, Paul undergoes an about-face. So thorough is Paul's transformation that he now sees his present manner of life as one that God had prepared for him before he was even born (1.15).[6] For someone with such an auspicious mission, however, Paul does not immediately take the front line in the Church's mission to the Gentiles. Instead he retreats for three years (1.17). Following that, he engages in conversation with others, most notably Peter and James (1.18). While it appears that Paul is proclaiming the gospel during this time (1.21–23), he also seeks confirmation of his interpretation of the gospel by fellow believers (2.2). In time (fourteen years according to 2.1), Paul's interpretation of the gospel is approved as is, by implication, Paul's character and authority as a faithful interpreter. It is this testimony from other faithful people that confirms Paul's character as a faithful witness.[7] Further, Paul maintains his position when others around him (Barnabas and Peter) vacillate under pressure from outside forces (2.11ff.).[8]

Scholars have disputed the accuracy of Paul's account and whether and how it can be related to the account given in Acts. What such inquiries miss, however, is that Paul related his biography in this way precisely because he thinks such an account testifies to his character as an interpreter of the gospel of Christ. Because Paul's interpretation (as well as his opponents' interpretation) of the gospel demands embodiment in the common life of the Galatian Christians, his character and authority as an interpreter are crucial to his interpretation and the Galatians' performance. Indeed, as Paul sees it, the continuing life of the Church as a faithful witness to God's activity in the calling of Abraham, in the death and resurrection of Christ, and in the continuing presence of the Holy Spirit in the community, depends on the Galatians' acceptance *and* embodiment of his interpretation. Hence, Paul's character is of no small account in this interpretive dispute.

Having reminded the Galatians of his character and authority as an interpreter of the gospel, Paul then addresses the character and experience of the Galatian Christians. He boldly asserts that they are in danger of becoming fools (3.1, 3). They risk turning the suffering they have already undergone in obedience to Christ into senseless pain (3.4). These disasters will come about if the Galatians fail to attend to the Spirit's activity in their midst. If the Spirit has already been at work in their lives, forming them to be the people of God, then their current life and character are proof of the truth of Paul's message. Recognition of what the Spirit has already done and is doing in their lives is the primary reason for continuing their allegiance to the gospel that Paul proclaimed to them. To turn away from Paul's interpretation of the gospel would be to deny their experience of the Spirit's work in their lives.

Thus, in chapters 1 and 2 Paul reminds the Galatians of his own character as a witness. He further notes how the character which the Spirit had formed in them confirms his interpretation of the Gospel (3.1–5). Only then does Paul turn to Scripture, directly entering into the interpretive dispute. What is at stake in the dispute is how the life, death and resurrection of Jesus stands in relation to God's call and sustenance of the people of Israel as attested in Scripture.

Scholarly accounts of Paul's use of Scripture have typically asserted that Paul reads the texts christologically.[9] Clearly, Paul reads Scripture in the light of his understanding and experience of Christ. As Richard Hays has recently shown, however, when Paul turns to his Scripture, particularly in Galatians, he finds the Church. That is, he interprets Scripture in ways that point to the Church as the new people of Israel. Further, Paul claims this transposition is not a capricious act of an arbitrary God. Rather, Paul's reading aims to show that the establishment of the Church as the new Israel is all part of God's continuous activity of calling and forming a people to be God's own. In this sense, then, Paul's interpretation is 'ecclesiocentric'.[10]

In Galatians Paul's interpretive interest is to show from Scripture that God always intended the Gentiles to be included in the people of God, *and* that God includes them without the precondition of obedience to the law. Paul's allusions to the Abraham story in Genesis form the basis for this assertion. The argument that Paul carries out in Galatians 3–4 is very complex, but in short it works like this: Paul relates God's promise to Abraham that all nations would be blessed in him as the basis for his argument (3.8). In Christ Jesus this promise is fulfilled and the blessing of Abraham is made available to the Gentiles (3.14, 29). Since God's promise is made before the giving of the law and is not conditional upon obedience to the law, its application to the Gentiles through Christ is not conditional upon obedience to the law (3.17ff.).

This point is then reiterated in Paul's 'allegorical' interpretation of the account of Abraham's two sons (4.21–26). Since Paul has already associated keeping the law with confinement and slavery (3.21ff.; 4.8ff.), he can then link the children of the bondwoman Hagar (who is Mount Sinai, the place where the law was given) with those who are attached to the law. 'The children of promise, according to Isaac', stand in contrast to these children of slavery.[11] The Galatian Gentile Christians are such children of promise since they are the visible fulfilment of God's promise to Abraham. These children of promise are free from the bondage imposed by the covenant at Sinai.[12] As Hays argues, 'Paul has not merely made a case for admitting the Gentiles into membership among the people of God; he has argued that the Genesis narrative is a veiled prefiguration of precisely the historical development that has now come to pass in the Gentile church.'[13]

To a contemporary critical exegete these are bold, even audacious, readings. This was also the way Paul's opponents probably perceived his interpretive activity. Paul himself might well have called them Spirit-inspired interpretations. For Paul, the truth of his interpretation is confirmed by the presence of the Spirit in the Galatian Church independent of obedience to the law. This presence of the Spirit is God's seal of approval on Paul's interpretation (3.14; 4.6).[14] In this way Paul's interpretive practice is doubly pneumatological. On the one hand, the interpretations themselves are Spirit-inspired. On the other hand, the confirmation of the interpretation is found in the presence of the Spirit in the community.

This would indicate that the presence of the Holy Spirit is a crucial criterion of faithful interpretation and performance.[15] We must admit, however, that it is often difficult to discern the presence of the Spirit in either the interpreter or the reading community. There is no litmus test one can perform to determine the presence of the Spirit. Rather, we are called to discern, to exercise practical wisdom. In such cases the character of the interpreter and the character generated in any particular community will be primary (though not exclusive) signs of the Spirit's presence. This means that Christians need to be people of character who are able to exercise practical wisdom. As we have already indicated, the growth of such practical wisdom is the dialectical result of previous interpretive practice and successful discernment and performance.

A community can never know beforehand whether it has the character to discern and to resolve interpretive disputes faithfully. We can, however, point to some examples where communities have lacked the character to hear the word of the Lord aright and see what the consequences of such failure were.

## INTERPRETIVE CONFLICT IN JEREMIAH

For Jeremiah, the continuing life of the people of God depends on being able to hear, to discern and to act upon the word of the Lord. This idea reaches its climax in chapter 31, where Jeremiah holds out the promise that one day God's law will be written on the hearts of the people of God. At that time, there will be no need to struggle over the word of the Lord, for all shall know God from the least to the greatest (see 31.34). Until that time, however, the people of God must engage in an ongoing struggle to discern the word of God rightly.

While the Book of Jeremiah displays many of the issues surrounding the reception of God's word, it would be impossible to find a system of interpretation or a series of formulae for determining the meaning of the word of the Lord. Rather, within the Book of Jeremiah we see that the ability to hear rightly and to act upon God's word depends upon having a certain type of character which exhibits particular virtues such as patience, hope and faith in Yahweh.[16] Further, Jeremiah indicates that the failure of the people of God to be people capable of hearing and doing God's word tends to lead them into violence and coercion.

One such episode illustrating this point is Jeremiah 27–29. This episode (which is really several episodes) shows that what is at stake in this interpretive conflict is not simply hermeneutical rectitude. Rather, the parties to the conflict recognize that the continuing life of the people of God lies in the balance. In this case, faithful interpretation is a life and death matter.[17] It is this close connection between hearing and doing God's word and the sustenance of the people of God that makes the failure to hear the word of the Lord a moral and not a hermeneutical failure. This connection also indicates why failure of this type makes violence such a likely result. With so much at stake, violence and coercion will always be close at hand.

Critics have often looked to these chapters, especially Jeremiah 28, in an attempt to develop criteria for determining a true prophet from a false one.[18] While this text may lead one to infer things about true and false prophecy in ancient Israel and while this is a potentially interesting critical issue,[19] it is important to recognize that the text exhibits little interest in the criteria for determining true and false prophecy. That is, this text is not primarily wrestling with the methodological question of how to determine a true prophet from a false one.[20] Rather, the primary conflict played out in these chapters concerns how the people of Judah are to respond to Nebuchadnezzar's conquest.

It seems clear that the situation presumed by these chapters is one in which Nebuchadnezzar, king of Babylon, has overrun Judah, deporting Jehoiakim, king of Judah, and much of the nobility.[21] Nebuchadnezzar has also taken away many of the Temple vessels. In the place of Jehoiakim, Nebuchadnezzar placed Zedekiah on the throne.[22]

How should Zedekiah and the other leaders of Judah respond to Nebuchadnezzar and the Babylonians? The implication of the warnings of 27.8, 15ff. is that there were those who advocated resistance.[23] This probably would have involved alliances with Egypt and the surrounding nations. The advocates of resistance felt that their only recourse was to rebel, to take up arms in the name of Yahweh and to trust Yahweh to deliver them. They wish to establish peace in the land through resistance. In their view, this is what Yahweh demands of faithful Jews. Repeatedly in chapter 27, however, Jeremiah warns against listening to these 'false prophets' (see 27.9, 14, 16).

Jeremiah has an alternative vision.[24] God informs him that politically things are going to stay pretty much as they are for quite a while. Nebuchadnezzar and his heirs are going to be in charge of Judah and all of the surrounding countries. Jeremiah and the rest of the people of Judah are to recognize this situation. They are to accept it and to order their lives accordingly. On God's instructions, Jeremiah makes a yoke and wears it as a symbolic expression of Judah's subjection to Babylon (27.2). Nebuchadnezzar is called Yahweh's servant. To rebel against him is to rebel against God. Failure to recognize this situation, or any attempt to resist this state of affairs, will result in total destruction (27.6–8).

This is not a pleasant message to bring from God. Nevertheless, its force is driven home by the fact that it is repeated in chapter 27 to the nations (vv.3–11), to Zedekiah (vv.12–15), and to the priests and all the people (vv.16–22). The warnings against the message of the lying prophets in chapter 27 are then concretely manifested in Jeremiah's conflict with Hananiah in chapter 28.

Chapter 28 begins with Hananiah relating a message for the people of Judah which claims to be the word of Yahweh. He asserts that within two years the exiles will return from Babylon, Jehoiakim will be restored as king, the Temple vessels will be reinstated, and the yoke of the Babylonians will be broken (28.3–4). Having just read about the message of the lying prophets in chapter 27, and in the light of the fact that Hananiah is subsequently called a liar, one might infer that the implication of

Hananiah's message is that the people of Judah should, in fact, take up some form of resistance to Nebuchadnezzar.[25] The difference between Jeremiah's and Hananiah's message is not simply the length of the exile. Rather, each interpretation of the word of the Lord demands to be embodied, but such embodiments would result in conflicting practices. Hananiah's interpretation urges resistance. Jeremiah speaks of building, planting and marrying (see 29.5–6). Hananiah's is a concrete example of the very message Jeremiah has just warned against.

No theory of textual meaning will resolve this interpretive dispute over the word of the Lord. Neither is it possible for the leaders of Judah simply to apply the criterion for discerning true from false prophecy outlined in Deuteronomy 18.21–22. Each prophecy demands a response in the present. The leaders of Judah could not sit back and wait to see which, if either, of these prophecies would come to pass.

In his defence, Jeremiah notes that this message at least stands in conformity with the message of previously recognized prophets (see 28.8–9). Even here, however, Jeremiah holds out the logical, though unlikely, possibility that Hananiah's prophecy may come true (28.6).[26] Hananiah, for his part, clearly sees Jeremiah's response as a sarcastic rejection of his prophecy. He shatters Jeremiah's yokes as a way of re-emphasizing his message. At this point Jeremiah retreats (28.11).

Hananiah's actions, however, provide Jeremiah with an occasion to express his message in even stronger terms as the broken yokes of wood are replaced by yokes of iron.[27] Further, Jeremiah brings a personal message for Hananiah. Jeremiah claims that God has not sent (*shelaka*) Hananiah but God will dispatch (*mishleka*) him soon.[28] Hananiah has made the people 'trust in a lie'. He has 'counselled rebellion against Yahweh'. Therefore, he will die within the year. The chapter closes by noting that two months later Hananiah is dead.

The text makes it painfully clear that Hananiah did not bring a word from Yahweh – quite the opposite. At the same time, the text gives us no reason to doubt his sincerity. Indeed, on the face of it, there is nothing particularly unorthodox in Hananiah's words. His message emphasizes the continuing faithfulness of Yahweh towards the people of Judah. It recognizes God's saving power and Yahweh's desire to establish peace in the land. Further, Hananiah puts himself at some risk by coming to Jerusalem and predicting in Zedekiah's backyard that Jehoiakim will be returned to the throne. This indicates that his message is neither self-serving, nor a reflection of the desires of the current structures of power.[29]

Someone who has read Jeremiah 27, however, is not surprised that Hananiah's words are characterized as deceitful. He urges the people to trust in a lie – an action typical of the prophets condemned at various points throughout Jeremiah (see Jer. 7).[30] Indeed, the judgement of Hananiah in chapter 28 is formally parallel to the judgements rendered against the lying prophets in 27.10, 14, 16.[31]

Hananiah's message seems to reflect the hope that the Lord will deal with Israel 'according to his wonderful deeds' (21.2). Such a hope rightly recognizes that Yahweh delights in lovingkindness. Hananiah's message fails, however, to incorporate the notion that God also delights in justice and righteousness (see 9.22–23).[32] Further, it is precisely in regard to justice and righteousness that the people of Judah have turned from Yahweh (see 5.20–31; 7.1–11; 21.12 ff.). Hananiah's failure is not so much one of failing to hear the word of the Lord as it is a failure rightly to know the Lord who issued the words.[33] He did not lead the people to 'trust in a lie' because the divine communication lines got crossed. Rather, his message indicates that he was not a person capable of rendering a truthful account of Yahweh.[34] It was this failure that made him incapable of speaking a true word from the Lord.

Hananiah is but one concrete example of a general problem afflicting the people of Judah throughout the Book of Jeremiah. They had adopted a partial, hence distorted, picture of Yahweh, refusing to have it corrected by Jeremiah. This distorted vision formed their lives in such a way that they became oppressors (see 5.28; 7.6; 21.12).[35] By failing to manifest the character appropriate to the people of Yahweh, they had in a real sense stopped being the people of Yahweh. This contributed to a further distortion of their understanding of Yahweh, making it increasingly difficult to hear a true word from the Lord. This theological and moral failure rendered them incapable of hearing Jeremiah's word from the Lord. Because they had become a certain type of people (a people other than the people of Yahweh), formed both by a specific (though corrupt) view of Yahweh, and by a failure to act in accord with Yahweh's justice, they were not able to recognize or to act upon the word of the Lord spoken by Jeremiah. As a result, the people of Judah turned to violence both against God's prophet, Jeremiah, and against God's instrument, Nebuchadnezzar. In short, their failures of character and interpretation contributed to further distortions in both their character and their interpretation. This downward spiral ultimately led them to act violently against those who pointed out their failings.

To be sure, Jeremiah's message is not an easy one to hear. Jeremiah was in the awkward position of telling a conquered people that God's will for them is to accept their position and, in effect, to do nothing to change it. Further, in chapter 29 Jeremiah is commanded to send his message beyond the confines of Judah to those Jews in exile in Babylon. They are not told to take up arms against the Babylonians, nor are they to try to subvert the state. Rather, they are told to build houses, to plant gardens, to raise families, and to seek the general welfare of Babylon.[36] They are patiently to wait for the Lord to work for them. In 29.11 Yahweh justifies this course of action by saying, 'For I know the plans I have for you . . . plans for welfare [shalom] and not for calamity, to give you a future and a hope.' Yahweh promises that the exiles will again be the people of God (29.12ff.).

Jeremiah's counsel is not one of inaction or indolence. The exiles are to build, to plant, to marry and to seek the welfare of Babylon. These activities are not based on pessimism, indifference, selfishness or cynicism. This is because in the course of doing all of these things the exiles are also waiting for Yahweh to act. Jeremiah bases his message to wait on the belief that Yahweh is Lord and, as Lord, Yahweh is capable of bearing our hope. Jeremiah's message is based on the faith that Yahweh has plans for shalom and not calamity. Such plans provide the people of God with a future and a hope. Jeremiah's faith in such a God is essential to his ability to hear and to pronounce the word of the Lord. This faith sustains the patience needed to wait for the Lord. The patience underlying Jeremiah's message is sustained by a particular faith in Yahweh – a God who has plans, who establishes and sustains our hope. This faith, in turn, forms Jeremiah into someone capable of bearing a word from the Lord.

Jeremiah's message ran counter to the way most of his contemporaries interpreted and proclaimed the word of the Lord. He was not, however, the harbinger of some new interpretive method. Rather, he indicates that being formed by a true knowledge of, and faith in, Yahweh is crucial to being able to hear, proclaim and enact the word of the Lord.[37] His interpretive conflicts with the 'lying prophets' and with Hananiah in particular illustrate that when the character, practices and habits of the people of God become distorted, there is little that a more refined interpretive method can do to enable them to hear the word of the Lord aright.

## A CONTEMPORARY DISPUTE: APARTHEID AND THE DUTCH REFORMED CHURCH IN SOUTH AFRICA

The rise of the theological and scriptural superstructure that supports apartheid within the Dutch Reformed Church in South Africa (DRC) provides a further example of the interrelationships between character and interpretation. This superstructure did not emerge in a full-blown form until this century, but its seeds were sown in the early and middle parts of the nineteenth century. Moreover, it does not appear that appeals to Scripture provided the primary justifications for apartheid.[38] Rather, the structures of apartheid were already deeply embedded in the practices and characters of the majority of DRC members. Scripture was only invoked after the fact to support what was already in place.

In the earliest days of its presence in South Africa, the DRC maintained a doctrine of the unity of the Church. At least in principle there could be only one Church for whites and blacks. In practice, the DRC manifested the sorts of class, cultural and educational divisions typical of other churches in the seventeenth and eighteenth centuries.[39]

The moves to establish separation within the Church began in the 1820s and 1830s. Ironically, these moves were the result of the Church's missionary activity. As blacks were evangelized and began to enter the DRC, they were eligible in principle to share in the Lord's Supper with their white brothers and sisters. This clearly angered some white DRC members who argued that their black sisters and brothers should have a separate service. This view was not unopposed. Several courageous pastors recognized the sin of excluding fellow Christians from the Lord's table on the basis of race.[40]

By the middle of the nineteenth century, the lobby in favour of separation within the Church had grown. The idea of one Church with separate services, or even separate congregations for 'members from the heathen', as new black converts were called, became very popular. This view was so strong that it threatened to undermine missionary activity among blacks. As a result, the Synod of 1857 resolved that

'although it was desirable that our members from the heathen be assimilated into existing congregations . . .' some who are 'weak' [read: whites] had opposed this and, therefore, '. . . impeded the propagation of Christianity among the heathen.' Thus, for the sake of reclaiming white support for mission work, synod decided that those Christians from the heathendom would henceforth '. . .enjoy their Christian privileges in a separate building. . .'[41]

The way this proposal is formulated – as a concession to the weak – indicates that it was intended to be a temporary situation. It also points out that the driving forces behind this decision are those of ecclesiology, evangelism and Church politics rather than scriptural interpretation.

It must be said, however, that when Paul talks about making concessions to the 'weak' in Romans 14.1ff. and 1 Corinthians 8.9ff. regarding the eating of meat sacrificed to idols, such concessions do not involve actively taking up a sinful position such as separating people from the Eucharist on the basis of race. One can only conclude that at this point the DRC was reading Scripture for itself rather than over-against itself. Texts such as 1 Corinthians 11.17–34, dealing with the manner in which Christians should eat the Lord's supper and the consequences of failing to eat worthily, and Gal. 2, seem to be much more appropriate to this situation.

Given this account of how separation within the DRC began, one might have expected steps to be taken to restore the unity of the Church. Since the problems were ecclesiological, one would have expected to see the Church undergo a collective process of conversation and discernment in order to win the 'weak' over to the truth. In fact, however, what began as a temporary situation gradually became solidified, rationalized and, ultimately, formalized into the doctrines of apartheid. What was initially sin was rationalized as weakness, and ultimately became the standard of righteousness for the Church.

Clearly, at every step of the way Scripture was invoked in the various arguments and discussions that took place in the DRC. It was only after apartheid had received its theological rationalization and was the *status quo*, however, that large-scale biblical justifications of this situation were offered. The most systematic and comprehensive of these accounts came out in 1974 under the title *Human Relations and the South African Scene in the Light of Scripture*.[42]

While the document cites many biblical texts, the position of the DRC rests on just a few key texts: Genesis 10–11; Acts 2.5 and 17.26.[43] From this rather thin base, the document claims that while God affirms the solidarity of humanity, God also ordains ethnic diversity. The document goes on to assert that this diversity can best be maintained by the practices of separation institutionalized in apartheid.

Without question, people ought to criticize this document for its selection and interpretation of Scripture. Others have made such criticisms elsewhere and in great detail.[44] Such criticisms are important, for they help to persuade people that the DRC's reading of Scripture does violence to the most powerful analogical constructions of the relation between Scripture and the South African situation. There are, however, two points related to our arguments in this chapter about character and interpretation which we ought to make.

First, even though the methodology and interpretive practice presented in *Human Relations and the South African Scene in the Light of Scripture* are flawed, there is a more fundamental flaw in the preparation of this document. This flaw lies in the character of the community that generated the document. This flaw is displayed in two self-deceptive acts. The first deception is in presuming that one can introduce separation based on race into the Lord's Supper without 'profaning the body and blood of the Lord' (1 Cor. 11.27). The second deception arises when such sin is excused (and ultimately rationalized into righteousness) by describing it as weakness. Any community that can countenance and consistently reaffirm these self-deceptions is not a community that we should expect to hear, interpret and embody the word of the Lord faithfully. Like Hananiah, those who provided the scriptural interpretation that supported this document in particular and the practice of Church-based apartheid in general caused their people to 'trust in a lie'. This failure is not simply a failure of interpretive method; it is a failure to have a well-formed character capable of faithful interpretive practice.

Our second point is directed at ourselves and all others who observe and cast judgement on various Christian communities in South Africa or elsewhere. This point is basically a reminder of how gradually and how simply such character distortions can enter into our own common life. Less than 200 years ago it was easy to find white American Christians who not only advocated the practice of enslaving Africans, but who found scriptural justification for such practice. In addition, our own congregations are often still as segregated as those in South Africa who accepted the views presented in *Human Relations and the South African Scene in the Light of Scripture*.

When distortions of character enter and deeply permeate the life of any Christian community, that community loses its ability to read Scripture in ways that would challenge and correct its character. Scripture simply becomes a mirror reflecting a community's self-deceptions back to itself disguised as the word of God. This is what happened to the DRC. It lost the ability to read Scripture over-against itself; it lost the ability to hear the critical, prophetic voice of Scripture. When this is the case, no amount of methodological sophistication can break the cycle in which a community with badly distorted character reads Scripture in ways that reinforce the community's character distortions.

By returning to the text of Jeremiah – chapters 42–43 in particular – we can see an example of this situation. While the people of Judah ultimately fail to hear the word of the Lord, we can see some of the conditions needed to break out of the cycle of distorted character reinforcing distorted interpretation.

## JEREMIAH 42–43 AND THE AMBIGUOUS NEED FOR A PROPHET

When we rejoin the story, Jerusalem has been destroyed. The best and the brightest people have either been killed or taken into exile. The Babylonians have appointed Gedaliah to govern those people who remain. Gedaliah sets up residence at Mizpah and urges those who come to him, 'Do not be afraid of serving the Chaldeans; stay in the land and serve the king of Babylon that it may go well with you' (40.9). In spite of the fact that this remnant began to experience some prosperity (40.12), we learn that Gedaliah is not universally loved. The Ammonites wish to assassinate him. They engage Ishmael, the son of Nethaniah, to do this. In spite of being warned, Gedaliah falls victim to Ishmael and his men.

Before the Chaldeans have a chance to exact reprisals upon the people, Johanan, the son of Kareah, gathers the people together and plans to lead them to Egypt. Johanan and his band approach Jeremiah, asking him to inquire of God whether they should go to Egypt or not.[45] Experience teaches that when the puppet who is ruling over you is assassinated, it is best to get out of town before the reprisals start. In spite of the obvious merit of this plan of action, the people want Jeremiah to find out what God wants them to do. In this light it is interesting that in 42.3 they ask Jeremiah to inquire of 'the Lord *your* God' rather than 'the Lord *our* God'.[46] Jeremiah corrects them by reminding them that Yahweh is the God of Judah and not simply Jeremiah's personal deity. Nevertheless, in spite of this distance they put between themselves and Yahweh, the people claim that they are willing to do whatever the Lord says 'whether it is pleasant or not' (42.6). It is clear from the next chapter, however, that they fully expect God to authorize their flight to Egypt. Jeremiah, for his part, commits himself to telling them the truth, the whole truth and nothing but the truth (42.4).

It takes ten days for Jeremiah to come back with a word from God,[47] and the message Jeremiah brings back runs against all expectation. It is, however, unequivocal: Fleeing to Egypt will bring the very thing they are trying to avoid; namely, defeat at the hands of the Babylonians.[48] Staying in the land will not only bring peace, but also restoration.[49] Jeremiah reiterates Gedaliah's admonition not to be afraid of the king of Babylon (42.11). This time, however, God gives a reason: 'For I am with you to save you and deliver you from his hand, I will also show you compassion, so that he will have compassion on you and restore you to your own soil' (42.11–12). Here, again, Yahweh ensures a future for the people if they are willing to let Yahweh bear their hope.

As chapter 43 begins we find out that this word from the Lord was not exactly greeted with great jubilation. In fact, Johanan and Azariah and all the other 'arrogant' men of Judah deny that this is what the Lord had told Jeremiah to say. They claim that Jeremiah is part of a plot to get them all killed (43.3). Indeed, they ironically accuse Jeremiah of telling a lie (*sheqer*), the very thing Jeremiah has accused so many others (including Hananiah) of doing (see 28.15; 23.25, 26, 32; 14.14; 29.9 *et al.*). Johanan and Azariah force all of the people of Judah, including Jeremiah, to march with them to Egypt. The text does not explicitly mention what happens. Instead, 43.8–44.30 narrates a whole stream of condemnations and curses against Egypt and Jewish communities in Egypt. As Carroll suggests, 'Those who go to Egypt, including Jeremiah and Baruch, now enter the area of the curses and cannot hope for anything other than a miserable life under Yahweh's curses.'[50]

Here, again, we find Jeremiah in the midst of an interpretive conflict regarding the word of the Lord. Unlike chapter 28, the text does not relate such a final and unequivocal resolution of the dispute between Jeremiah and the people led by Azariah and Johanan. We are, however, left with the strong impression that in Egypt things turned out as Jeremiah foretold. As with chapter 28, there seems to be a close connection between Jeremiah's character and convictions, on the one hand, and his ability to hear the word of the Lord on the other hand. For example, throughout the book of Jeremiah, and particularly in this instance, the prophet manifests courage in proclaiming difficult words from the Lord. This courage stands in sharp contrast to the arrogance of Johanan, Azariah and the other men of Judah. Jeremiah's courage is sustained by hope in a God who saves (42.11–12).

The arrogance of the Judeans is a mixture of fear and authoritarianism. It reflects a failure of hope. The courage needed to hear, to proclaim and to act on the word of the Lord recognizes that God does not exist simply to underwrite the plans we make for ourselves. Rather, sometimes the word of the Lord directly contradicts our own plans, hopes and interpretations. In these cases, faithfulness to God demands that we exhibit the courage needed to stand against the prevailing wisdom of the day, particularly when that 'wisdom' is based on arrogance, fear and coercion, and not on faith and hope. Such courage comes from having a character shaped by and devoted to hearing the word of the Lord.

Jeremiah's proclamation of the word of the Lord is also sustained by his very particular faith and hope in Yahweh. As we noted above, his faith is in a God who plans shalom for us (29.11ff.), in a God who claims, 'I am with you to save you. . .' (42.11–12). Such a faith inspires and confirms hope in God's deliverance. This hope for...s the basis of the courage that allows Jeremiah to proclaim his message in the face of the arrogant men of Judah on the one hand, and the armies of Babylon on the other hand.

If and when a community becomes unable to hear the word of the Lord rightly because of deeply embedded character distortions, it gets caught in the downward spiral of mutually reinforcing failures of character and interpretation. In such situations, a prophet like Jeremiah, one who can stand on the fringes of that community and yet address the word of the Lord to the community in its own language, may be the only one who can break the downward spiral. In the case of the DRC, such a prophet was Beyers Naudé. Beginning in the 1950s, Naudé called his fellow Dutch Reformed Christians to recognize the errors that had become deeply embedded in their life, worship and interpretation. He exhibited the interpretive virtues of Jeremiah as he addressed a people whose character was informed by a distorted picture of God. Unfortunately, he met with a response similar to Jeremiah's. Because of his actions, the South African government banned Naudé in 1978.

We should not forget that the people of Judah failed to respond to Jeremiah's message. Further, while the situation in South Africa remains to be resolved, it is not clear that the DRC has reformed itself in accord with a true knowledge of God. When prophets from God achieve ambiguous results (at best), we should beware of ever finding ourselves in such a position that only a prophet can speak the word of God faithfully to us. The examples of history would indicate that when the people of God have got into a situation in which their primary need is for a prophet, then the situation may already be too far gone.[51]

This would indicate that forming a courageous and faithful character such as the one that enables Jeremiah to hear, to speak and to act on the word of the Lord is essential for *all* those people of God who, following Jeremiah, struggle to hear the word of God aright. Developing this type of character is not merely a personal matter. The consistent failure of the people of Judah to recognize and act upon Jeremiah's word from the Lord indicates that a character nurtured by (among other things) courage, patience and hope is not for prophets only. No matter how many prophets there were in Judah, ultimately it was the people as a whole who corporately had to act upon the word of the Lord.

Hence, for Christians, the struggle to nurture, discipline and form a Christ-like character engages the whole people of God. Such a struggle is grounded in the conviction that by being formed in this way we will be better able to hear God's word for our particular situations.


## CONCLUSION

Our aim in this chapter has been to take up our earlier comments on the importance of character in Christian ethics and to show some of the ways in which issues of character are related to interpretive disputes. While we cannot possibly indicate all of the ways in which character and interpretation interrelate, we have argued that scriptural interpretation is not only bound up with particular social contexts, it is also related to the character of the interpreters. The example of Paul's conflict with opponents in Galatia makes this point.

A Christ-like character, however, is not a commodity that can be purchased; neither can it be put on and taken off at will. It is formed over time through disciplined attention to our thoughts, words and practices. That is why in earlier chapters we have argued that Christian communities need to establish spaces in which believers can have their characters formed and informed by a true knowledge of God.

Issues of character can also be the driving force behind interpretive disputes within Christian communities. The conflict in Judah between Jeremiah and Hananiah illustrates this. Moreover, failures of interpretation and corrupt character are mutually reinforcing. In such situations, communities lose the ability to read Scripture over-against themselves in ways that challenge current ways of thinking and acting. The gradual rise of doctrinaire apartheid within the Dutch Reformed Church in South Africa shows how this can happen to a community of Christians.

When corrupt character becomes deeply ingrained in the fabric of a community's life, it undermines that community's ability to interpret Scripture faithfully. This can become a vicious circle in which corrupt character and distorted interpretation mutually reinforce each other. Such cases often require the perspective of a prophet who can stand against the various corrupting elements of a community's life while at the same time faithfully addressing the word of the Lord to that community in its own language. The cases of Jeremiah and Beyers Naudé point this out.

As we noted, however, Jeremiah and Naudé are ambiguous examples to the extent that they both brought true words from the Lord to their communities which their communities systematically ignored. This ambiguity indicates that all Christians must struggle to become people of character who engage in faithful interpretation. When Christian communities fail to form their members in this way, they open themselves to the possibility of becoming communities in need of a prophet, just like the people of Judah in Jeremiah's day and the DRC in our own time. Of course, such an injunction must lead us to consider our own situation in Britain and North America. We should not presume that we do not need a prophet, lest such a presumption render us unable to hear the word of the Lord.

In addition to character formation, Christians need to cultivate active dialogues with outsiders so as to avoid the interpretive self-deception into which the people of Judah and the DRC fell. As we noted above, when a community's failures of character and interpretation become deeply entrenched, there is little they can do to extricate themselves from this situation apart from hearing the voice of a prophet. As we will argue in the next chapter, however, cultivating the skills and habits of talking with outsiders will help to avoid this situation. It is to this that we now turn.

## NOTES

1. The presumption that character is unimportant to professional biblical critics is sustained by the fact that virtually all professional interpretation aims to further abstract ideals like 'scholarship as such'. In order to serve scholarship, professional interpretation need not be performed or embodied as a part of a community's ongoing life. In fact, because 'scholarship' is such an abstract and

elastic notion it is not clear how one furthers scholarship except by producing more books and articles. Thus, the very abstractness of the idea of scholarship leads to the reduction of interpretation to a commodity. One might further argue that professional scholars have a vested interest in maintaining this situation. For if any discipline started to define scholarship in narrower and/or more concrete ways it would risk excluding a large proportion of its current members.

The one occasion when character is important for professional interpretation is when the ideal of 'scholarship as such' is threatened by things like plagiarism and the falsification of evidence. In these cases the scholarly community is both interested in the character of interpreters and attempts to form the virtues of scholarly integrity in young scholars.

2. For an account of the work of basic ecclesial communities in Brazil, see Leonardo Boff, *Ecclesiogenesis*, tr. Robert Barr (London: Collins; Maryknoll, NY: Orbis, 1986). For an account of biblical interpretation in these communities see Carlos Mesters, *Defenseless Flower*, tr. Francis McDonagh (Maryknoll, NY: Orbis, 1989).

3. This is not a claim unique to biblical interpretation. Character is an important feature in assessing the persuasiveness of any rhetor. For an interesting discussion of this point, see David S. Cunningham's Ph.D. Dissertation, 'Faithful Persuasion: Prolegomena to a Rhetoric of Christian Theology' (Duke University, 1990).

4. George Howard's *Paul: Crisis in Galatia*, SNTSMS 35 (Cambridge: Cambridge University Press, 1979) and T.L. Donaldson's 'The Curse of the Law and the Inclusion of the Gentiles: Gal. 3.13–14', *New Testament Studies* 32 (1986) pp. 94–112 both emphasize the importance of the inclusion of the Gentiles as a theme of Galatians.

5. Although he does not use the language of character, John Schütz has also recognized the close connection between the recognition of Paul's gospel and the recognition of Paul's apostolic authority. 'In both passages [Gal.1 and 1 Cor.15] Paul's thought involves a radical identification of the gospel and the apostolic agent. Such an identification can lead to an explication of the "gospel" (as interpretation of tradition) in terms of apostolic experience.' See *Paul and the Anatomy of Apostolic Authority*, SNTSMS 26 (Cambridge: Cambridge University Press, 1975), p. 135.

6. This is a claim also made by the Servant in Isaiah 49.1 and by Jeremiah in Jeremiah 1.5.

7. See also Acts 10.26ff., where Barnabas attests to Paul's character to a wary church in Jerusalem.

8. For a useful discussion of the role of Paul's autobiography in Galatians 1 and 2, see Beverly Gaventa, 'Galatians 1 and 2: Autobiography as Paradigm', *Novum Testamentum* 28 (1986), pp. 309–326.

9. See, for example, Richard Longenecker, *Biblical Exegesis in the Apostolic Period* (Grand Rapids, MI: Wm. B. Eerdmans, 1975), pp. 104ff.

10. This term is used by Richard Hays in *Echoes of Scripture in the Letters of Paul* (New Haven, CT: Yale University Press, 1989) pp. 84ff. Much of what we say in the following paragraphs is indebted to Hays.

11. See C.K. Barrett, 'The Allegory of Abraham, Sarah and Hagar in the Argument of Galatians', in *Essays on Paul* (London: SPCK; Philadelphia, PA: Westminster, 1982), pp. 154–69. See also Hays, *Echoes of Scripture in the Letters of Paul*, pp. 111ff.

12. Note that the contrast here is not between the old covenant and the new, but between the old covenant and the older covenant (see Hays, *Echoes of Scripture in the Letters of Paul*, p. 114).

13. ibid., p. 116.

14. In fact, Paul interprets the presence of the Spirit as God's promised blessing of the Gentiles (see ibid., p. 110).

15. Recall our argument in Chapter 3 for the contemporary significance of the Holy Spirit for a Christian community's interpretation of Scripture.

16. One of the critical issues that has re-emerged in the cluster of recent commentaries on Jeremiah concerns the extent to which we can recover the life and preaching of the historical Jeremiah. While we would be even more skeptical about abilities to uncover the historical Jeremiah than we are about our abilities to uncover the historical Jesus, we do not deny the conceptual legitimacy of this enterprise. For our part, nothing we say about Jeremiah or his prophecy should be taken as a reference to a historically reconstructed Jeremiah. See in particular Robert P. Carroll, *Jeremiah: A Commentary*, OT Library (London: SCM; Philadelphia, PA: Fortress, 1986); William Holladay, *A Commentary on the Book of the Prophet Jeremiah, Chapters 1–25*, Hermeneia (Philadelphia, PA: Fortress, 1986); William McKane, *A Critical and Exegetical Commentary on Jeremiah*, Vol. 1, ICC (Edinburgh: T & T Clark, 1986). See also Walter Brueggemann's comments on this trend in 'Jeremiah: Intense Criticism/Thin Interpretation' *Interpretation* 42 (1988), pp. 268–80.

17. As we have already indicated, such extreme circumstances as the people of Judah find themselves in make issues of interpretation and character far more poignant (though no less important) than they might otherwise be. The cases of Latin America and South Africa could just as easily make this point in the modern world.

18. See, for example, Thomas W. Overholt, *The Threat of Falsehood*, Studies in Biblical Theology 16 (Naperville, IL: Allenson, 1970); or the very different approach of Henri Mottu in 'Jeremiah v. Hananiah: Ideology and Truth in Old Testament Prophecy', in *The Bible and Liberation*, ed. Norman K. Gottwald (Maryknoll, NY: Orbis, 1983), pp. 235–51.

19. It is, however, interesting to note that while the Septuagint identifies Hananiah as a *pseudoprophētēs* the Masoretic Text simply designates him as a *nabi*.

20. See Brevard S. Childs, *Old Testament Theology in a Canonical Context* (London: SCM; Philadelphia, PA: Fortress 1985), pp. 139ff. At

this point Childs is followed by Gerald Sheppard, 'True and False Prophecy within Scripture', in *Canon, Theology and Old Testament Interpretation*, eds G. M. Tucker, D. L. Petersen and R. Wilson (Philadelphia, PA: Fortress, 1988), pp. 262–82.

21. These three chapters raise a host of critical problems. For example, there is confusion in the text over the time at which the events in chs. 27–29 took place. Chapter 27 verse 1 sets a scene at the beginning of Zedekiah's reign. The events of chapter 28, which must have happened soon after those in 27, are said to occur in the fifth month of the fourth year of Zedekiah's reign. While there is a logical need to have the events in these chapters occur shortly after one another, there seems to be no way to determine which is the correct date. For various attempts to resolve these problems see: John Bright, *Jeremiah*, The Anchor Bible (Garden City: Doubleday, 1965), p. 199; Carroll, *Jeremiah: A Commentary*, p. 538; Ernest W. Nicholson, *The Book of the Prophet Jeremiah*, The Cambridge Bible Commentary, 2 vols. (Cambridge: Cambridge University Press, 1975) vol. 2, pp. 30–1; Artur Weiser, *Der Prophet Jeremia*, ATD (Göttingen: Vandenhoeck and Ruprecht, 1955), p. 251 n.1.

22. In spite of the fact that most Hebrew manuscripts of 27.1 mention Jehoiakim as the king, this would seem to be a re-copying of 26.1 (so goes the argument of J. A. Thompson, *The Book of Jeremiah*, NICOT [Grand Rapids, MI: Wm. B. Eerdmans, 1980], p. 529 n.1 and most others). The verse is absent in the Septuagint and the rest of the text assumes Zedekiah is the recipient of the prophecy (see 27.3, 12, 16).

23. See Daniel Smith, 'Jeremiah as Prophet of Non-Violent Resistance' *Journal for the Study of the Old Testament* 43 (1989), p. 102.

24. Walter Brueggemann argues that the people of Judah's vision of Yahweh's relationship to the people of God and Jeremiah's alternative vision are both encapsulated in 9.22–23. See 'The Epistemological Crisis of Israel's Two Histories (Jer. 9.22–23)', in *Israelite Wisdom: Theological and Literary Essays in Honor of Samuel Terrien*, eds J. Gammie, et al. (Missoula, MT: Scholars Press, 1978), pp. 85–108, esp. 88ff.

25. See Smith, 'Jeremiah as Prophet of Non-Violent Resistance', p. 102.

26. Carroll, *Jeremiah: A Commentary*, sees Jeremiah's response in verse 6 as a straightforward expression of his hope that Hananiah's prophecy is correct (see p. 544). Reading chapter 28 in conjunction with the previous chapters, particularly chapter 27 (a practice Carroll is not willing to adopt but that readers of the final form must adopt), would lead us to read verse 6 as a somewhat sarcastic response (see Nicholson, *The Book of the Prophet Jeremiah*, vol. 2, p. 37). At the very least, reading Jeremiah 28 in the light of Jeremiah 27 would lead one to follow Childs, in *Old Testament Theology in a Canonical Context*, who claims that in verse 6 Jeremiah holds out the possibility that God has the freedom to change his mind (see p. 139).

27. It is not clear who makes these yokes. The Septuagint indicates that

it is Yahweh (I). The Masoretic Text says it is Hananiah (you).

28. There seems to be a play here on the Hebrew word *shalak*.
29. Carroll, in *Jeremiah: A Commentary*, p. 549, makes this point against Mottu's Marxist reading of the passage in 'Jeremiah v. Hananiah: Ideology and Truth in Old Testament Prophecy'.
30. See Overholt's discussion of this point, in *The Threat of Falsehood*, pp. 1–23.
31. Childs, in *Old Testament Theology in a Canonical Context*, notes the formal parallels between these two chapters (see p. 138).
32. See Brueggemann, 'The Epistemological Crisis of Israel's Two Histories', pp. 91ff., who says that this text '. . . articulates the basic issues that finally cannot be avoided in Judah . . .' (p. 99).
33. See Childs, *Old Testament Theology in a Canonical Context*, p. 139, who says, 'In sum, the issue at stake is theocentric . . .'
34. Carroll is right to complain that scholars have often been 'so eager to praise Jeremiah and denigrate Hananiah that they read into the text much that is simply not there' (*Jeremiah: A Commentary*, p. 549). But on the same page he also claims that the text 'chooses not to attack his character'. It seems to us, however, that the charge of leading the people to 'trust in a lie' is precisely an attack on Hananiah's character. Further, while chapter 28 does not give any direct reasons as to why Hananiah's message is a lie and represents 'rebellion against Yahweh', one could make inferences as we have done from previous chapters in the text to address this issue. In other words, while we have read things into our account of chapter 28 which are clearly not there, we would argue that such inferences and assumptions we have made in regard to chapter 28 are justified by other portions of Jeremiah. Carroll's unwillingness to read chapter 28 in conjunction with the rest of Jeremiah leaves him with little to say on this issue.
35. See Overholt, *The Threat of Falsehood*, who writes, 'Their error was probably not so much that they denied that the covenant carried with it certain conditions, as their view of salvation (based on their knowledge of election) as guaranteed did not permit them to take these conditions seriously' (p. 22).
36. The images of building and planting are often (though not solely) used in Jeremiah to illustrate the future blessings Yahweh will bestow on a renewed Israel (see 18.7–8; 24.6–7; 27.11; 31.27–28; 42.9–10; 45.4). See also R. Bach's article 'Bauen und Pflanzen', in *Studien zur Theologie der alttestamenlichen Uberlieferungen*, ed. R. Rendtorff and K. Koch (Neukirchen, Neukirchener Verlag, 1961), pp. 7–32. Smith, 'Jeremiah as Prophet of Non-Violent Resistance', draws on Deuteronomy 20, 28 and Isaiah 65 to note that the combination of the images of building, planting and marrying are images of peaceableness, that Jeremiah's letter is a declaration of peace (see pp. 100ff.).
37. Jeremiah, like the Servant in Isaiah 49, has the sense of having been chosen by God and formed for his special role as prophet to the nations (see 1.5).

38. This is not to deny that Scripture underwrote the rationale for the Afrikaner colonization and subjugation of the native peoples of southern Africa in the seventeenth and eighteenth centuries. In this respect, the Afrikaners were not substantially different from other colonial movements of the time. Rather, our point is more narrowly focused on the rise of the structures of apartheid as they arose in the DRC and spread to the wider society.

39. See Johann Kinghorn, 'The Theology of Separate Equality: A Critical Outline of the Dutch Reformed Church's Position on Apartheid', in *Christianity Against Apartheid*, ed. Martin Prozesky (New York: Macmillan, 1990), p. 58.

40. For a brief account of the rise of apartheid in the DRC which mentions some of its opponents see Chris Loff, 'The History of a Heresy', in *Apartheid is a Heresy*, eds John de Gruchy and Charles Villa-Vicencio (Grand Rapids, MI: Wm. B. Eerdmans, 1983), pp. 10–23.

41. This quote from the Synod minutes and the comment come from Kinghorn, 'The Theology of Separate Equality', p. 58. There is a telling contrast between the means used to resolve a dispute by this Synod and the means described by Paul in Galatians 2.

42. Dutch Reformed Church Publishers, Cape Town-Pretoria. This is the official English translation of the report *Ras, Volk en Nasie en Volkereverhoudinge in die lig van die Skrif*, which was accepted by the DRC's General Synod in October 1974.

43. The major scriptural arguments occur in sections 9–14.

44. See particularly the articles by Willem Vorster and Douglas Bax in *Apartheid is a Heresy*, eds de Gruchy and Villa-Vicencio, pp. 94–111 and 112–43.

45. Carroll, in *Jeremiah: A Commentary*, p. 715, notes that with the destruction of Jerusalem, Jeremiah now seems able to intercede for the people (see 7.16; 11.14; 14.11).

46. The Septuagint (chapter 49) reads 'our God' in verse 4 and omits 'your God' in verse 5.

47. It is interesting that both here and at chapter 28 a period of time elapses before Jeremiah returns with a word from the Lord.

48. Compare the similarities between the calamities mentioned here and those of 29.18.

49. As in chapter 29, God uses images of building and planting to illustrate this restoration.

50. Carroll, *Jeremiah: A Commentary*, p. 724.

51. Of course, there is a sense in which the prophetic task is always incumbent upon Christian communities. Our comment is directed to a situation in which a community's overarching need is for a prophet.

# 5

## Listening to the Voices of Outsiders: Challenges to Our Interpretive Practices

Thus far we have focused on interpretation *within* the community of believers. Given what we have said so far, one might claim that our positions are at best introspective and at worst sectarian. Hence, in this chapter we will argue that one of the characteristics of a community of wise readers is an openness to outsiders. There are both conceptual and theological reasons why this attitude of openness must characterize Christian interpretation of Scripture.

Without ears to hear the voices of outsiders, we can forget that now 'we know in part and we prophesy in part...now we see in a mirror dimly' (1 Cor. 13.9, 12). Our interpretations can take on pretensions of permanence. When our communities fall prey to this greatest of interpretive temptations, it is often only the voice of outsiders that can set us right. If we have not taken the time to cultivate the skills, habits and dispositions that allow us to hear the voices of outsiders, we will fall into a situation of interpretive arrogance. That is, we will deceive ourselves into thinking that our words are God's word. The exercise of power and coercion will characterize our communities. Conformity rather than faithfulness will be the standard used to judge our lives. If nothing else, then, our awareness of our own tendencies towards interpretive self-deception should compel us to learn to listen to outsiders.

Any community that cuts itself off from engagement with outsiders deprives itself needlessly of a crucial resource for living and interpreting faithfully. This is not to say that outsiders will always be right, will always have the best interpretation, or will always be able to call us to truthful living. If this were the case, there would be little sense in developing a community whose interpretive practices will always be undermined by outsiders. Further, there may be times when a community needs to stand against the prevailing wisdom of those outside the community if it is to live faithfully before the Triune God. All of these qualifications, however, do not undermine the claim that if the people of God hope to read and enact the Scriptures faithfully in the various contexts in which we find ourselves, we will need to listen to (if not always follow) the words of the outsiders we encounter.

If we are to listen to the voices of outsiders, we need to be able both to recognize outsiders and to learn how to listen to their strange voices. Of course, who counts as an 'outsider' depends on who you are and where you stand. Even so, in this chapter we will identify some outsiders common to contemporary North American and British Christian communities. Further, we will provide some rules of thumb for listening to outsiders. We will begin by identifying four types of outsiders. Our list, however, is suggestive rather than exhaustive.

## OUTSIDERS WHO GOVERN OUR COMMON LIFE

Given what we have said so far, it is not surprising that we claim that there is a sense in which Scripture is an outsider in relation to the Christian community. The force of this claim, however, is not to complain about the fact that Scripture is marginal in many aspects of the Church's life and practice. Nor do we wish here to lament the level of biblical illiteracy among Christians today. Both of these states of affairs are causes for concern. They work to make and to keep Scripture a foreign text, a closed book. They do not, however, represent the way we want to think of Scripture as an outsider. This is because even if these contemporary problems were corrected, there would still be a sense in which Scripture is and should be an outsider.

Scripture functions as an outsider for any particular Christian community when it is read 'over-against ourselves'. We have already dealt at some length with this notion in Chapter 2. In addition, in the next chapter we will show more concretely how Dietrich Bonhoeffer embodied this attitude. For now, we simply want to emphasize that to read Scripture over-against ourselves is to allow it to challenge our presuppositions and established interpretations. To allow Scripture to be an outsider is to recognize that this side of the Kingdom our interpretations are provisional, always open to revision. The aim of treating Scripture as outsider, however, is not interpretive paralysis. Rather, the goal of seeing Scripture as an outsider is the maintenance of interpretive humility and openness to hearing the voice of Scripture afresh.[1] This can only happen when we realize that Scripture is not simply us in disguise; it should not be a mirror we use to reflect our prejudices back to us as the word of God.

When we refuse to recognize this difference between our common life and Scripture, when we fail to recognize the sense in which Scripture is an outsider, our interpretations become petrified and unyielding. Unless we allow Scripture to examine us and to challenge our interpretive practices we will lose the ability to act faithfully in the new contexts in which we find ourselves. This is precisely the phenomenon that Bonhoeffer confronted in Germany during the rise of the Nazis.

In addition to Scripture, there is another outsider who governs the common life of Christian communities. In fact, this outsider is the governor of all Christian communities, namely the resurrected Christ. The story of Jesus' appearance to the two disciples on the road to Emmaus (Luke 24.13–35) is perhaps the best example of the interpretive importance of this outsider.

While Jesus is still a stranger to these two mourning and perplexed disciples, he interprets the Scriptures for them in ways that make their 'hearts burn' within them (see 24.27, 32). This is not, however, where the story ends. The resurrected Christ does not remain simply an outsider who helps the disciples interpret Scripture. Instead, he first becomes their guest as they invite him to share a meal with them. Then, 'in the breaking of the bread', he is made known to them as the risen Lord (24.35).

In this passage an outsider enables the disciples to see in new ways. Christ's activity transforms their outlook from confusion and disappointment to joy and hope. Their experience of being taught by the resurrected Christ, the outsider, and their joy at recognizing the resurrected Lord in the breaking of bread enable them to read their Scripture (which is not precisely our Scripture) in a new way.

Likewise, we must also look to the resurrected Christ to help us interpret and perform Scripture faithfully. Yet, like the disciples on the Emmaus road, we may find that the resurrected Christ engages us as an outsider who, in the breaking of the bread, also becomes our friend.

## OUTSIDERS IN OUR MIDST

The second type of outsider Christian communities may encounter, and to whom such communities should pay particular attention, are those members who are estranged from our common life. These outsiders are part of us, yet because of currently unresolved interpretive disputes they have become alienated from our common life. One such example of this type of outsider is homosexuals within the Church.

This issue has frequently polarized Christians, making discussion and debate difficult if not impossible. The intensity of the feelings about homosexuality among many North American and British Christians is odd, particularly since these same people are seemingly apathetic about such issues as material and social justice, the environment and racism. This situation is even more perplexing when we realize that these latter issues are not so much matters of conflicting interpretations as of disobedience, of a sinful unwillingness to perform Scripture when it is clear that it will cost us some of our material comforts and closely guarded prejudices.

Such disobedient attitudes may also be present in debates over the role of homosexuals in Christian communities. Nevertheless, there are also issues of real interpretive controversy.[2] People prayerfully committed to ordering their lives in accordance with their interpretation of Scripture are honestly divided over these issues. At such a juncture the need for people to exercise all of their interpretive (and other) virtues in an open conversation with all the concerned parties could not be more acute. Such conversations, however, have been the exception rather than the rule. On this (and other) issue(s), we have needed to embody the conversational openness and discernment characteristic of the conference in Jerusalem related in Acts 15.[3] Instead, we have most often replicated the posturing and self-serving debate characteristic of contemporary partisan politics.

We have tended to make outsiders of those whose very presence in our churches makes this a live issue of scriptural interpretation for us. We have pushed them to the margins of our church life, forcing them to shout their message to us from the few safe havens they have been able to find. Typically, Christian communities have responded to issues of homosexuality and the role of homosexuals in the Church by making these fellow believers into outsiders.

Alternatively, in some more recent circumstances homosexual believers have sought to coopt the discussion, shaping the discourse in such a way that it would be impossible to disagree with their position without being identified as 'homophobic' or 'heterosexist'. In such situations, believers who disagree with this perspective have become outsiders who are to be ignored. Regardless of which side coopts the discourse, the result is the creation of outsiders whose voices are silenced.

It is not our aim to offer decisive readings of particular scriptural texts which would once and for all settle these debates. Rather, our concern is that Christian communities in general (and our two churches in particular) seem unable to engage in the sort of multi-sided conversation needed to bring about faithful (albeit provisional) interpretations and performances of Scripture in regard to these particular issues. In order to do so, we must carry on a conversation within the body of Christ in which there are no outsiders. To the extent that we have already made some members of the body outsiders, the body of Christ must engage in the offering and receiving of forgiveness and reconciliation. This is not to deny, however, that in the light of a faithful discussion, any particular members of the body might become subject to communal discipline if they are unwilling to be reconciled to the body's reading and performance of Scripture. In such cases, they would make themselves outsiders. We must remember, however, that discipline follows rather than precedes both discussion and the offering of forgiveness and reconciliation (see Matt. 18).

In addition to establishing a forum for conversation, communities should avoid some of the interpretive pitfalls that have often characterized discussions of these issues. First, we must remember that all of Scripture is canonical (i.e. the norm and standard to which our conversation must conform) and must be addressed in its diversity. Writings such as the Pastoral Epistles cannot be ruled out of the discussion simply because they might not have been written by Paul. The text is canonical, the apostle is not.

On the other hand, we should not presume *a priori* that any particular text or texts must be determinative. Indeed we may judge that the most important texts for evaluating homosexual practice are ones that do not explicitly address homosexuality. After all, we should not make judgements about homosexuality in isolation from other convictions Christians ought to hold about marriage, family, sexuality and community.

Just as judgements about homosexuality cannot be made in isolation from other convictions and practices, we must remember that 'homosexuality' is not a single issue. We need to recognize that the extent to which we can map practices described in the Bible on to practices operating today is a matter of dispute. This is not a question of whether or not we 'know' more today about homosexuality than the biblical writers did. This issue concerns whether and to what extent the biblical practices and attitudes construed as 'homosexuality' are similar to practices and attitudes currently described as 'homosexuality'. The vocabulary of the Bible may overlap with our own, but because we often use words differently we may end up talking about different things.

For example, some scholars relying on linguistic studies of the relevant vocabulary and an understanding of a variety of social practices in the Greco-Roman world have argued that it is more accurate to describe the practices condemned in I Corinthians 6.9 with a term like 'pederasty' than with a blanket term like 'homosexuality'.[4] One might further argue that Scripture does not explicitly address the question of faithful monogamous relationships between people of the same sex. While such interpretive options do not resolve the issue, these possibilities need to be considered in any discussion among Christians.

Clearly, nothing we have said here will decide the concrete interpretive disputes that have arisen and will arise around the issue of homosexuality. Neither have we discussed how to integrate 'readings of the world' drawn from other fields of inquiry into our 'readings of the texts'. Rather, given that questions about 'homosexuality' have produced intense interpretive conflict among Christians, our aim has been to point out that the discussions so far have succeeded primarily in creating a caste of outsiders within particular Christian communities. This is a sinful situation. Our desire to see the body of Christ united must lead us to act in ways that will rectify this situation. Only then can a community hope to arrive at a faithful reading and performance of Scripture. Only then can we expect to hear the voices of these outsiders.

So far we have talked about Scripture, the resurrected Christ, and homosexuals in the Church as outsiders. In each case we have discussed how any particular community might address these outsiders. The tasks involved in becoming able to discern the identity of, and to hear and converse with these outsiders, require us to develop and embody both critical and moral virtues.[5] However, we should not expect that simply refining our exegetical techniques will enable us to hear the voices of outsiders any better. Rather, the type of refinements that have to take place are related to our character and the political constitution of our communities.

## OUTSIDERS BEARING A FAMILY RESEMBLANCE

In each of the preceding cases, we identified outsiders who want to be intimate participants in our faith and practice. The fact that they approach us as outsiders is a reflection of the moral and political inadequacies of our particular Christian communities. Jews, however, are a different sort of outsider to Christian communities. They are outsiders bearing a family resemblance. Our Scriptures, while not identical, overlap. Moreover, Christians and Jews share some common history – unfortunately often a tragic history marred by the sinfulness of Christian anti-Semitism. For these reasons alone, Christian readers of Scripture should be particularly interested in hearing the voices of Jews.

It might seem strange that we look to the Jews as outsiders to whom we should listen in the light of some of our Scriptures. For example, in Matthew's Gospel the story of the Syro-Phoenician woman (which we will discuss below) serves as part of a polemic against Jews (at least Jews who do not follow Jesus). In fact, in several places Matthew uses Gentile outsiders to show Israel what their faith should be like. The centurion in Matthew 8.5–11 manifests a faith that Jesus 'had not found in Israel'. It seems clear that at least part of Matthew's aim is to polemicize against those Jews who don't believe in Jesus by presenting these Gentile exemplars of faith. It is also likely that this is one of many strategies in Matthew's Gospel which provided the Gospel's first readers with ammunition and sustenance in their conflicts with those Jews who did not recognize Jesus as the Messiah.

These textual comments might lead one to claim that the Jews are precisely the outsiders to whom we should not listen. The role of the Church in aiding and abetting Hitler's 'final solution', however, should remind us of the sin we fall into when we consider outsiders to be expendable and/or unnecessary for our own faithful interpretation and performance. Particularly in the wake of the Holocaust, then, Christians need to listen to the Jews.[6]

Because Jewish and Christian Scriptures and ways of identifying God overlap, Jews have a discourse that can address Christians with particular immediacy. They can point to an unredeemed world to challenge Christian claims that the Messiah has come. Further, they can use our own language to call us to live into our character.[7] In addition, their readings of the Hebrew Bible can be vitally important for Christians' readings of the Old Testament.

Nevertheless, there is no virtue in denying that we are outsiders to one another. Nearly two millennia of history, and of Christian anti-Semitism, now ensure that the Jews are not really us in disguise. However, it is beneficial, at least to the Church, to engage these particular outsiders in a conversation over the interpretation and performance of our Scripture, hoping both that they will talk to us and that they will help us to be more faithful.


## OUTSIDERS WHO ARE COMPLETE STRANGERS

So far we have talked about outsiders who for various reasons all have some particular interest in talking to us. Because of this, their importance for our interpretive practice and our common life generally is more or less self-evident. It is less clear that we should be interested in conversing with outsiders who are complete strangers to us. Nevertheless, we want to argue that Christians should develop the skills and dispositions needed to talk with strangers. Further, we contend that such conversations can be more than polite attempts to pass the time with those strangers among whom we find ourselves. Such conversations can actually be crucial to the way Christians interpret and perform Scripture.

Scripture itself provides some of the best reasons we can give for adopting such a perspective – in particular, Jesus' encounter with the Syro-Phoenician woman related in Mark 7.24–30 and Matthew 15.21–28. We will argue that these stories provide us with exemplary accounts of why Christian interpreters of Scripture must engage with outsiders. We will begin by looking at Jesus' encounter with the Syro-Phoenician woman as related in Mark. To do this we will need to set this story in the larger context of Mark's Gospel.

From the beginning of Jesus' public ministry in Mark, he has been moving around Galilee preaching and teaching about the Kingdom of God. He has been calling people to follow him and forming them to be disciples in spite of their repeated failures; healing diseases; doing battle with Satan; and engaging in controversy with fellow Jews – most particularly the Pharisees.

As Mark 7 begins, Jesus is engaged in just such a controversy with the Pharisees and some of the scribes from Jerusalem (7.1). As Mark relates it, the issue at hand concerns whether one should eat with unwashed hands. The Pharisees ('and all the Jews') observe the 'tradition of the elders' (7.3) and wash, the disciples do not. The issue here is not one of physical hygiene, but of ritual purity (7.4).[8]

The Pharisees' emphasis on 'the traditions of the elders' allows Jesus to contrast their rigorous adherence to human tradition with the sophistry they use to avoid 'the commandment of God' (7.6–13). He claims that their hypocrisy is rightly characterized by Isaiah 29.13: 'This people honour me with their lips, but their hearts are from me; in vain do they worship me, teaching human precepts as doctrines'(NRSV).[9]

Having directly confronted the Pharisees, Jesus then addresses the crowds following him on the issue of purity. He tells them to 'listen to me all of you, and understand: there is nothing outside a person that by going in can defile, but the things that come out are what defile' (7.14–15, NRSV).

Only when he is alone with his disciples does Jesus unpack this cryptic utterance for them (and us readers).[10] What people eat cannot defile them because it does not enter their hearts. The food simply enters the stomach and is passed on out of the system, which Mark takes as a declaration that all foods are clean. Rather than what they eat, it is what comes out of people – words and deeds – that defile them. This is because such things come from the heart, which, as the quote from Isaiah shows, is the basis for one's relationship to God (7.14–23).[11]

Before we find out the reaction of the Pharisees, the crowd or the disciples, we read that Jesus leaves the scene of confrontation. In fact, he leaves Galilee altogether to go into the region of Tyre and Sidon. Here Jesus is a foreigner, a stranger. The text indicates that he wished to remain that way, to be anonymous, to be left alone.[12] This was not to be (7.24).[13] Immediately upon hearing about him, a woman with a daughter who had an unclean spirit came and fell at Jesus' feet (7.25).[14] Before anything else happens, we are told that she is 'a Greek, a Syro-Phoenician by birth'.[15]

As this encounter unfolds, the woman is a voiceless character. The action is narrated in the third person. We learn, however, that she is asking Jesus to cast out the demon from her daughter. Jesus, who speaks for himself, replies, 'Let the children be fed first,[16] for it is not good to take the children's bread and throw it to the dogs' (7.27).[17] Jesus' recourse to cryptic, indirect speech is similar to his earlier address to the crowds in 7.15. Unlike the disciples, however, this woman immediately catches the force of Jesus' reply to her request. Jesus is refusing to heal her daughter.

Jesus' response is both surprising and uncomfortable. It is surprising to the extent that a woman on her own, evidently with few resources and with a sick daughter, seems to be just the type of person Jesus delights in healing.[18] In spite of the fact that this woman transgresses cultural codes regarding male/female contact, we can recall that in Mark 5 Jesus healed the destitute and desperate woman with a haemorrhage who transgressed the same boundaries by initiating contact with Jesus. Further, he has already performed what would seem to be a more difficult miracle in raising Jairus's daughter from the dead.

Moreover, this woman is not like those from Jesus' home region who are offended by his wisdom and power and for whom Jesus cannot act with his characteristic power 'because of their unbelief' (6.1–6). The very fact that she seeks out Jesus when he does not wish to be found attests to her faith and determination. She seems much more like those in Gennesaret, whose sick Jesus readily healed (6.53–56). Almost everything a reader of Mark would have encountered in the first seven chapters of the Gospel would lead one to think Jesus would be more than willing to heal this woman's daughter.

The one detail that might explain Jesus' unwillingness to perform this act of healing is related in 7.26. That is, this woman is a Greek, a Syro-Phoenician by birth.[19] She is not one of the 'children' to whom Jesus' bread is to be offered. The assumption behind the Markan passage, which is made explicit in Matthew's account, is that the 'children' are the 'lost sheep of the house of Israel'. The upshot of Jesus' comment is that because she is not an Israelite, he refuses to heal her daughter. While Jesus is an outsider in the regions of Tyre and Sidon, he refuses to heal this woman's daughter because she is an outsider to the people of Israel.

The manner in which Jesus makes this plain adds to our surprise and discomfort.[20] In spite of the best exegetical gymnastics of Christian commentators, one cannot escape the conclusion that Jesus equates this woman with 'the dogs', and that he aims both to deny her request and to insult her.[21] Clearly, the image reflected in Jesus' words is of a household scene. Nevertheless, the contrast between 'children' and 'dogs' is clear, as is the identification of the Jews with the children and the Gentiles with the dogs. Only those with both a distorted picture of Jesus' piety and a complete lack of familiarity with the Gospels will be surprised that Jesus is capable of barbed speech. What is surprising is that the insult seems so gratuitous. Further, it comes so soon after Jesus has both relativized Jewish purity codes and has closely linked what comes out of the mouth with what is stored in the heart (7.20–23).[22]

At this point in the story Jesus has completely closed himself off from this woman and her plight because she is an outsider. The woman, however, refuses to let the matter rest. At verse 29 she finally gets her own voice. Without disputing the justice of Jesus' position, without responding to his insult, she takes his response and turns it on its head to her own advantage: 'Lord, even the dogs under the table eat the childrens' crumbs.' Her pluck and wit break down Jesus' resistance and he tells her to go her way and that the demon has left her daughter (7.29).[23] Before making some comments about the interpretive importance of listening to outsiders, we should first look at Matthew's side of the story.

In Matthew's account (like Mark's) this story immediately

follows a dispute with the Pharisees and scribes over the 'tradition of the elders'. In Matthew, however, we read that the Pharisees understood the force of Jesus' response to them and were offended. The Pharisees' offence is a cause of concern for the disciples. Jesus tells his disciples not to be worried about the Pharisees. They are blind guides (15.12–14).

For their part, however, the disciples (who are not blind) have failed to understand that 'People are not defiled by what goes into their mouth, but what comes out of the mouth defiles them' (15.11; see also 15.15–20). In response to this confusion, Jesus gives the same basic explanation as in Mark.

Following this, Jesus removes himself to the region of Tyre and Sidon. Matthew links Tyre and Sidon together to describe one area (Mark separates them). At several points in the Old Testament this pair of cities is identified as Israel's enemy.[24] Unlike Mark, we are not told that he wishes to travel incognito. Rather, we are presented with the picture of a Jew who has entered enemy territory. This impression is further reinforced when the woman who comes to meet him is identified as a 'Canaanite', the traditional enemies of the Israelites.[25] This woman asks Jesus to cast a demon from her daughter. While the woman's plight is the same as in Mark's account, her interchange with Jesus has some subtle differences.

First, from the very beginning in Matthew she has her own voice and speaks for herself. She cries out, 'Lord, Son of David, have mercy on me…' (15.22). Although she is not a Jew, she uses a very Jewish form of address.[26] While she may be an outsider, her speech makes it clear she is not the enemy we had been led to expect.

On the other hand, Jesus remains silent in the face of her pleas (15.23). While Jesus is silent, the disciples are not. In response to her continued pleas, the disciples ask Jesus to 'send her away' (15.23). The force of this request is not immediately clear. Do they wish Jesus simply to rebuff the woman and thus send her away? Or do they want Jesus to grant her request and, in doing so, get rid of her?[27] Some light is shed on this question when we look at Jesus' response, 'I was sent only to the lost sheep of the house of Israel' (15.24). This response is directed at the disciples and not the woman.[28] As a response to the plea to send the woman away, it really only makes sense if Jesus assumed that the force of the disciples' request was that Jesus should heal the

woman's daughter. This is not to say that the disciples are moved
by compassion for the woman. They simply see her as a nuisance.

While this discussion between Jesus and his disciples is going
on, the woman interposes herself, crying 'Lord help me' (15.25).
Finally, Jesus addresses her. His discourse is as surprising and
uncomfortable as in Mark.[29] In Matthew, however, there is no
ambiguity about the reasons for Jesus' response. The way Matthew
has told the story, it is clear that this woman's status as a Gentile,
an outsider, is the reason why Jesus refuses to grant her request.[30]
In response to this, the woman replies with the same pluck and
wit as in Mark. Mark emphasizes that her reply itself is the reason
for Jesus granting her request. Matthew sees great faith implied in
the woman's remarks. It is on account of this faith that Jesus heals
her daughter (15.28). After reading these stories, one is compelled
to say that while Jesus is the one who performs miraculous works
of healing, the real import of these stories lies with this woman
and her example of pluck, courage and faith in the face of Jesus'
rejection of her as an outsider.[31]

We are accustomed to thinking that Jesus' ministry is characterized by his willingness to reach out to those considered by
his contemporaries to be outsiders. He is the one who eats
with publicans and sinners (Mark 2.15–17). In contrast to his
contemporaries, Jesus is the one who includes Zacchaeus as a
child of Abraham (Luke 19.9). Throughout the Gospels Jesus'
ministry to the 'lost sheep of the house of Israel' involves bringing
in those sheep whom others considered to be irremediably outside
the fold.

When he is in Tyre and Sidon, however, Jesus is in a new
context, in a foreign situation. It is not clear how he should
carry on his mission to the outsider. Based on his comments
about eating with unwashed hands, one might argue that Jesus
should not treat this woman as an outsider simply on the basis of
her ethnic origin.[32] In this passage, however, both Matthew and
Mark make it clear that Jesus' mission is to the people of Yahweh.
Initially, in the case of this woman, Jesus drew the line. She was
a true outsider and thus beyond the purview of Jesus' activity. In
spite of Jesus' initial attitude, however, this woman's persistent
wit and faith enable him to see her as one to whom healing was
due. In so doing, this woman, this outsider, helps Jesus act in a
manner consistent with the character he has already displayed. As

Gail O'Day notes, 'The Canaanite woman knows who Jesus is and holds him to it.'[33]

Matthew and Mark make the common point that Jesus is helped to see in new ways and to act in a manner consistent with his character through the ministrations of an outsider. This story exemplifies the importance of outsiders to the life and ministry of Jesus.

If Christians are to read in communion faithfully, we must learn from this story about the importance of strangers. Like the Syro-Phoenician woman, strangers can both demonstrate what faithful action in any given context would look like and hold us accountable to our character in those contexts.


## HOW TO LISTEN TO OUTSIDERS

Even if we are persuaded of the importance of listening to outsiders, it is by no means clear *how* we should listen to outsiders. We should not assume that listening to outsiders is a skill that can be picked up simply by an act of the will. The first step is recognizing the importance of listening to the various outsiders we encounter. If, however, someone is really an outsider, talking with them and listening to them is going to be difficult. We need to *learn* to listen to outsiders, and such learning takes time. Learning to listen to outsiders requires the acquisition and refinement of a wide range of conversational skills and dispositions.

The *ad hoc* and contextual nature of conversation make it impossible to specify in advance what skills and dispositions we will need. Even so, we can offer some rules of thumb that are particularly important for engaging outsiders. Like all rules of thumb, ours are general and abstract, but they do set up some guidelines that may enhance our abilities to hear the voices of outsiders.


### THE OUTSIDER IS *NOT* US IN DISGUISE

One of the things that would stifle our ability to hear the voices of outsiders is to presume that they are basically like us. In such cases we presume that, if only outsiders could stand in our shoes, they would agree with us, they would think like us, they would be us.

Given this presumption, our engagement with outsiders would primarily be directed towards getting them to recognize that if they could only see things from our perspective, they would agree with us. The underlying assumption behind this form of engagement is that outsiders are not capable of having their own coherent yet different systems of belief and practice. When we begin from this presumption, conversations with outsiders basically become attempts to make them see the error of their ways.

The problem with this approach is not the fact that the people who employ it hold strong convictions about the truth of their beliefs. One would expect Christians to be committed to the truth of their central convictions. The problem with this manner of engaging outsiders is that it is not really a conversation. In such a view, outsiders are not given their own voice because we refuse to acknowledge that they may have coherent beliefs different from ours. As a result, conversation (which is at least a two-party affair) becomes impossible.

A variation on the arrogance of the presumption that the outsider is essentially us in disguise is the conviction that everyone basically believes the same things. In this view, we engage outsiders in the hope that through dialogue both parties will be able to help each other scrape away the contingent and inessential elements of their faith and practice with the aim of finding an essential core of shared belief.

It might even be argued that for those who hold this view, there are no outsiders. That is, deep down we are all members of one community divided only by the contingencies of history and location. Another form of this view might argue that we are all outsiders. That is, we are all, to different degrees, alienated from that common core truth which unites us all. We engage each other as a form of therapy, hoping to overcome this alienation.

On the one hand, those who practise these forms of engagement with outsiders rightly recognize that there is some overlap between various systems of belief and practice. They also correctly recognize that within all systems of belief and practice some elements are more important than others. Some are essential, some are not.[34]

On the other hand, those who engage outsiders in this way start to go wrong when they assume that the inessential elements in any system of belief and practice are contingent particularities that can be scraped away without loss to the essential universal core of the system. What such people fail to recognize is that particularity permeates the whole system. Even the most essential convictions of Christian faith and practice are cast in very particular terms. This is even true of Christian claims that have universal applicability. For example, the claim that all people are created in the image of God – a claim with universal applicability – attains its intelligibility for Christians because of its relation to a particular story about the creative activity of a specific character whom Christians have come to identify as the Triune God.

Failure to recognize this particularity will lead Christians to distort these convictions into something alien to Christianity. Instead of coming to agreement with outsiders over a universal common core of shared belief, those who engage outsiders on the basis of this assumption are bound to come up with some hybrid system of belief and practice that faithfully represents neither party's views.[35]

Rather than engage outsiders from the presumption that they are basically us in disguise (or the variant view that both outsiders and us are the same people wearing different disguises), we must extend a certain interpretive charity to outsiders if we are to learn to hear their voices. The basic assumption of this interpretive charity is that outsiders' systems of beliefs and practice have a coherence and integrity of their own. Further, we violate that integrity if we presume either that outsiders basically hold our views (albeit in a less coherent form) or that we all hold basically the same views (except for the contingencies that have become encrusted on our systems of belief and practice over time). In the fractured world in which we live, the presence of outsiders who are willing to talk with us is a rare gift. The least we can do is extend this interpretive charity to them.

Following this rule of thumb about how to listen to outsiders need not entail that we abandon our own convictions. Neither does it mean that we should not try to persuade outsiders of the superiority of our own views. While we need to avoid arrogance in our conversations with outsiders, we also need to avoid false humility. Instead, we should engage outsiders in an attitude of trust. Such trust hopes that, as Jesus found, engagement with the outsider can help us in our various contexts to read and enact Scripture in ways that are more faithful than they otherwise would have been.

## THE OUTSIDER IS NOT COMPLETELY ALIEN

The point of this rule of thumb is to counter our tendency to consider the voices of outsiders so foreign as to be virtually unhearable. In such cases, we view the distance (whether temporal, spatial or conceptual) between ourselves and outsiders to be so great as to make engagement with them at best irrelevant, and at worst impossible. Of course, any particular engagement with outsiders may turn out to be irrelevant. This is, however, a judgement that can only be made retrospectively and on a case-by-case basis. There is no *a priori* theoretical reason that renders engagement with outsiders irrelevant or impossible.

Further, even to be able to recognize someone as an outsider means that we recognize and presume a certain amount of common ground between us and them. This is even implied in the very designation of particular outsiders as 'them' rather than 'it'.[36] That is, all disagreements of the type that would lead us to consider someone an outsider depend on a large amount of common assumptions and dispositions. If these assumptions and dispositions were not already in place, there would be little chance of finding a common issue about which to disagree. To have recognized someone as an outsider is already to assume that they share things in common with us. This is because only those who share enough with us to be able to disagree about certain common subjects can be counted as outsiders. Anything else is truly alien.[37] To consider someone an outsider rather than an alien presupposes that there is sufficient common ground to make comparison between them and us possible.

Even in cases where we initially seem to encounter true aliens, the familiarity that comes with the passage of time and the extension of interpretive charity may cause us to reconsider these aliens as outsiders or even friends. The chances of encountering a true alien are very small indeed. The odds against finding true aliens and the contingent possibility of finding friends among those we initially considered alien should work together to rule out any presumption against engaging outsiders on the grounds of being too foreign to be heard. This does not, however, mean that it is by any means an easy task to engage the outsider. This point leads us to a third rule of thumb which is a corollary of the second.

## TRANSLATING ALIEN TALK IS NOT EASY, BUT IT IS POSSIBLE

While the outsider (even to qualify as outsider) is never completely alien, it is certainly the case that some outsiders address us in 'foreign' tongues. This is true even among those who ostensibly speak the 'same' language. We all have had conversational experiences where we seem to talk around each other because, in an important sense, we are *not* speaking the same language. As we noted above with the reference to homosexuality, our descriptions and readings of the world may differ so greatly from other people's that conversation breaks down. If we are to overcome this situation, we will need to learn to engage in processes of translation.

The very obvious difficulties involved in translation may lead us to think that the language of some outsiders is too distant (whether temporally, spatially or conceptually) to be translatable into our language. In other words, the difficulties of translation may lead us to claim that it is actually impossible to engage some outsiders.[38]

We reject this view that some outsiders' language is simply untranslatable. Our arguments against this view, while technical, are analogous to those we used against viewing any outsider as completely alien. In short, the argument is this: for any group of expressions to which we ascribe the term language there must be sufficient overlap with our own expressions to allow analogies to be drawn and translation to begin. If there were absolutely no parallels between another group's expressions and our own, we would lack sufficient reason for ascribing the term 'language' to their expressions. In such a case, there would then be no issue of translation and translatability.

Having granted that there are sufficient parallels between our expressions and those of another to allow translation to take place in principle, there is no reason to think that the actual task of translating the language of outsiders into our own will be simple or straightforward. Further, translatability in principle does not entail that translation is possible at any particular time. As Jeffrey

Stout has argued, 'If, at a given time, a proposition expressible in one language, $L_1$, is not expressible in another, $L_2$, this need not be so at some later time. $L_2$, after all, can be developed hermeneutically.'[39]

As an example of this view of translation, consider the following scenario that Stout presents. The scenario illustrates the steps needed to carry out translation between a group of Kantian explorers who have been lost in the jungles of Brazil since 1831, the Modernists, and The Old World Corleones who have led an equally isolated life in Sicily:

> The Corleones go on at length about purity, honor, and role-specific virtues and obligations. The Modernists do not exactly dissent from propositions employing such concepts. They do not even entertain such propositions. Instead their moral talk is about human rights, respect for persons, freedom and what individuals (not strictly defined by their social roles) morally ought to do.... Most moral propositions entertained in one culture have no analogues in the other. They don't share enough common ground, it seems, to disagree with, or to translate, each other's sentences.[40]

On their first encounter with each other, the Corleones and the Modernists may well find it impossible to talk to each other. They may be tempted to deny that the other group actually has a language. If, however, they are more charitable, they may simply claim that they do not at present have the conceptual and linguistic resources to translate the other's language. By the very fact that they have encountered one another, however, each culture has opened itself to interpretive innovation.

Such innovation is the first step in making the untranslatable translatable. Stout notes that 'Nothing in the nature of cultural diversity itself prevents one culture from developing the means for expressing an alien culture's moral proposition or grasping their truth.'[41] Once this innovation has taken place, there is nothing in the nature of language itself to keep the Corleones and the Modernists from translating each other's languages:

> No doubt we shall need extended commentaries and cautionary remarks as well as translations of sentences to render Corleone moral discourse fully intelligible in our books about it. And if we encounter a concept for which we have no natural equivalent, we may need to begin by transliterating a term or two while writing longer commentaries and footnotes, thicker thick descriptions.[42]

The long, slow task of translation from scratch begins as we start to assume similarities and posit analogous expressions.

If we are willing to start from scratch, to learn a new language, to keep our initial assumptions of similarity open to revision, to translate a short phrase with a long explanatory paragraph to make all of its presuppositions clear, to exert sufficient effort and to spend sufficient time over the task, then all languages worthy of the name are translatable.

We have argued that the continued health of Christian interpretation and performance of Scripture depends on engaging outsiders. Such engagement will often require translation of the 'foreign' tongues of outsiders. Clearly, however, not all Christians have the specific skills needed to translate outsiders' discourses. Indeed, there may be cases where Christians have to rely on the linguistic skills of non-Christians. This means that there may be occasions when some Christians may encounter certain outsiders whom they cannot engage as they would like. Over time, however, the work of translators can remove this constraint. Until such time as that happens, we must charitably assume that these outsiders whose language we cannot understand may have something important to say to us about the reading and enacting of Scripture. They may even turn out to be friends.

These rules of thumb and their various corollaries are not designed to be exhaustive. They simply set out some basic parameters within which Christians can exercise their conviction that outsiders may have something very important to tell us about how we should read Scripture and live in the world.

## CONCLUSION

In this chapter we have discussed the interpretive importance of outsiders. They can challenge and correct our interpretive practices, reminding us of the provisionality of our readings and performances. Thus Christians wishing to read in communion must learn to engage and to listen to the voices of outsiders. Towards that end, we have identified some of the outsiders encountered by contemporary North American and British

Christians. In addition, we have provided some general rules of thumb for how to listen to the voices of outsiders.

The life and death of Dietrich Bonhoeffer exemplifies the awareness of how important it is to listen to outsiders. More generally, Bonhoeffer's practices of interpreting and performing Scripture provide a significant instance of the importance of reading in communion. Thus we now turn to an exploration of Bonhoeffer as a performer of Scripture.

## NOTES

1. While it may seem odd to speak of Scripture having a voice, Paul envisions Scripture (the Septuagint) as a voice that speaks in Galatians 3.8; 4.30. Speaking of this Pauline phenomenon Richard Hays notes, '...the text is reckoned as a knowing voice that has the power to address the present out of the past – or to address the past about the present, in such a way that readers, overhearing, may reconceive the present'. See his *Echoes of Scripture in the Letters of Paul* (New Haven, CT: Yale University Press, 1989), p. 107.

2. To get the flavour of this controversy among professional biblical scholars, see Victor Paul Furnish, *The Moral Teaching of Paul*, rev. ed. (Nashville, TN: Abingdon, 1985); Robin Scroggs, *The New Testament and Homosexuality* (Philadelphia, PA: Fortress, 1983); and Richard Hays, 'Relations Natural and Unnatural: A Response to John Boswell's Exegesis of Romans 1', *Journal of Religious Ethics* 14 (1986), pp. 184–215. For discussions of the wider issues, see D. Sherwin Bailey, *Homosexuality and the Western Christian Tradition* (London: Longmans, Green and Co., 1955) and John Boswell, *Christianity, Social Tolerance, and Homosexuality* (Chicago: University of Chicago Press, 1980).

3. Luke T. Johnson both reflects on the decision making procedure in Acts 15 and urges its embodiment for communal discussions of this particular issue in his book *Decision Making in the Church* (Philadelphia, PA: Fortress, 1983).

4. See, for example, Furnish's discussion of this issue in *The Moral Teaching of Paul*, pp. 67–72.

5. Discerning who is an outsider in our midst is a contingent judgement related to the shape of particular Christian communities. For example, in many circumstances the poor might constitute a group who have been made into outsiders in our midst (cf. Amos 4, Mt. 25.31–45).

6. One of the best accounts of how Jewish/Christian conversations should take place is found in Bruce Marshall's currently unpublished

1989 AAR paper, 'Truth Claims and the Possibility of Jewish-Christian Dialogue'.

7.  For an example of a Jew doing so, see Michael Goldberg's *Jews and Christians: Getting Our Stories Straight* (Nashville, TN: Abingdon, 1985).

8.  For a detailed discussion of Jewish purity laws, particularly as they relate to Mark 7, see Randall P. Booth, *Jesus and the Laws of Purity*, JSNTS 13 (Sheffield: JSOT Press, 1986). Booth (pp. 189–205) argues that the sort of washing observed by these Pharisees (and not all Pharisees observed this practice) was a work of supererogation. That is, it was not strictly required by levitical purity codes. This is presumably why Mark identifies the basis for this practice as lying with the 'tradition of the elders'.

9.  The quotation from Isaiah 29.13 cited here seems closest to the Septuagint.

10. See 4.10ff., 9.28ff., and 10.10ff. for other occasions where Jesus privately teaches the disciples away from the crowds.

11. This connection to the Isaiah quote is made by Robert Guelich, *Mark 1–8:26* Word Biblical Commentary (Waco, TX: Word Publishing, 1989), p. 378.

12. Mark 1.35, 1.45 and 6.31 also mention occasions where Jesus sought respite from the crowds.

13. In Mark 3.8 we read that Jesus' fame had reached Tyre and Sidon.

14. This is the same posture Jairus adopts in Mark 5.22 to request healing for his daughter.

15. This double identification leaves no doubt about her Gentile status. This contrasts sharply with the Gerasene demoniac and the deaf/mute in Mark 7.31–37 who are not identified as either Jew or Gentile. Commentators have assumed, however, that since these healings took place outside of Galilee these two were Gentiles also.

16. One should not make too much of the word 'first'. While the notion of feeding the children 'first' holds out the possibility that in time the dogs may be fed sometime in the future, there is no question about the fact that Jesus is refusing to heal this woman's daughter at the time she initially asks him.

17. The only other times Mark uses *chortazō* are in the feeding stories of chapters 6 and 8. Some scholars have argued from this that the use of the verb here is meant to interpret the two feedings. The feeding in 6.34ff. is a feeding of Jews and the second in 8.1ff. is a feeding of Gentiles. This section as a whole, then, would be an implicit argument for the legitimate presence of both Jews and Gentiles at the eucharistic meals of the early Church. The two main proponents of this view are T. A. Burkhill, *New Light on the Earliest Gospel* (Ithaca, NY: Cornell University Press, 1972), pp. 82ff. and B. van Iersel 'Die wunderbare Speisung und das Abendmahl in der synoptischen Tradition', *Novum Testamentum* 7 (1964), pp. 188–90. The main point against this view is that in 7.27 *chortazō* has nothing to do with literal eating. See also Guelich, *Mark 1–8:26*, p. 386 for

further criticisms of this view.

18. We infer that she has no close male relative because if she did, it would have been more appropriate for this male to approach Jesus. For a woman to approach a man in the first century Mediterranean world was to transgress a whole range of cultural codes of appropriate behaviour. For a discussion of this see Bruce Malina, *The New Testament World* (Atlanta: John Knox Press, 1981), pp. 42ff. See also the comments of Sharon Ringe, 'A Gentile Woman's Story', in *Feminist Interpretation of the Bible*, ed. Letty Russell (Oxford: Basil Blackwell, 1985), p. 70.

19. If, as most commentators assume, the demon-possessed man Jesus encounters in that vaguely identified place known as the 'region of the Gerasenes' is a Gentile (5.1ff.), then Jesus' response to this woman is even more inexplicable. While we do not have the space to argue the point here, however, there are good textual reasons for thinking that this character is not a Gentile.

20. Of course *our* surprise and discomfort are precisely the reverse of the discomfort that first-century Jewish readers would have felt in hearing this story. For them, the surprise is not that Jesus rejects the woman, but that in the end he succumbs to her overtures. We are indebted to Richard B. Hays for pointing this out.

21. The Old Testament is full of examples of pejorative uses of 'dogs' (see Deut. 23.19; 1 Sam. 17.43; 24.14; 2 Sam 9.8; 16.9; 2 Kings 8.13; Prov. 26.11; Sir. 13.18). The harshness of these words is not mitigated by the fact that the diminutive (i.e. 'Little dogs') is used here.

22. Burkhill's view in *New Light on the Earliest Gospel* (p. 82) that in 7.24ff. the doctrines of 7.1ff. are put into practice seems oblivious to the fact that Jesus initially refuses to heal the woman's daughter and would never have done so were it not for her wit and persistence.

23. In the story that immediately follows this one (7.31–36), Jesus returns from the region of Tyre and Sidon to the area of Decapolis. Here a man who was both deaf and had a speech impediment is brought to him. Jesus heals him without question. There is nothing specific in the text to identify him as a Jew. This very silence, however, contrasts with Mark's clear identification of the Syro-Phoenician woman. When this silence is coupled with Mark's use of the Aramaic *Eph'phatha* and the allusions to Isaiah 35 in 7.37, it seems most likely that this man was a Jew.

24. See Isaiah 23; Joel 3.4. J. P. Meier, *Matthew* (Wilmington, DE: Michael Glazier, 1980), p. 171, intimates that the pairing of Tyre and Sidon is designed to show that Jesus stays within the boundaries of Israel. There is little reason to accept this. In the light of Matthew's designation of the woman as a Canaanite, it would appear that the stage is set in such a way as to show Jesus in enemy territory confronted by an enemy.

25. By this point in time, however, there were no Canaanites around. Matthew is using an anachronistic designation to present Jesus as a

Jew in enemy territory confronted by an enemy. See Gail O'Day, 'Surprised by Faith', forthcoming in *Listening*, manuscript p. 2.

26. Of course, from the beginning of Matthew's Gospel with the appearance of the Magi, Matthew has portrayed occasions of Gentile recognition of the Jewish Messiah.

27. Floyd Filson, *The Gospel According to Saint Matthew* (San Francisco: Harper & Row, 1960), p. 180, lists this as a possible interpretation. Robert Gundry, *Matthew* (Grand Rapids, MI: Wm. B. Eerdmans, 1982), p. 312, denies this as a possible reading. Gundry's position is based on an unpersuasive argument about Matthew's use of the verb *apoluō*. In Matthew 18.27 one finds *apoluō* used exactly as it is here with the view of sending someone away by granting their request.

28. This is the position of Gundry, *Matthew*, p. 312, and O'Day, 'Surprised by Faith', manuscript, p. 6. Jesus' response echoes his command in 10.5–6 for his disciples to go only to the 'lost sheep of the house of Israel'.

29. Matthew does not have the phrase 'Let the children be fed first'.

30. In 8.3 Jesus healed a centurion's servant. The only real difference on these two occasions is that this one not only involves Gentiles, but takes place in Gentile territory. While Matthew clearly characterizes Jesus' mission as a mission to the Jews, by including these two stories he shows that Gentiles with faith can receive mercy as well.

31. O'Day, 'Surprised by Faith', manuscript, pp. 4–5 emphasizes that the woman, rather than Jesus, is the real protagonist in the story.

32. Numerous commentators note that the significance of placing the story of the Syro-Phoenician woman immediately after Jesus' dispute with the Pharisees over purity is to show Jesus putting his discourse about purity into practice (see especially Burkhill, *New Light on the Earliest Gospel*, pp. 82ff.). Jesus' initial response to the woman, however, shows that it is not clear (at least to Jesus) how one should apply his general statements about purity when one is in a very different context.

33. O'Day, 'Surprised by Faith', manuscript, p. 16; also Ringe, 'A Gentile Woman's Story', p. 71.

34. The list of what is essential and what is not will vary from context to context and from time to time. In addition, the exact specification of these elements at any point in time will always be a matter of debate. Nevertheless, it seems reasonable to assume that at any given time and in any given context one could change some elements of Christian faith and practice without distorting one's identity as a Christian.

35. When these views are applied to interreligious discourse it results in what Gavin D'Costa calls the 'Pluralist Paradigm'. The chief example of this paradigm is found in the work of John Hick. In criticizing this view D'Costa says, 'The pluralist seems to view truth-claims from other religions as a priori partial claims, which can then be reconstructed within a larger pluralist complementary model. Surely this type of dialogue can damage the integrity of the truth-claims made by other religions in denying their status

as the ultimate claims about the way things are. The charges of arrogance and triumphalism may curiously rebound back upon the pluralists who direct these same charges at exclusivists.' *Theology and Religious Pluralism* (Oxford: Basil Blackwell, 1986), p. 38. See also *Christian Uniqueness Reconsidered: The Myth of a Pluralistic Theology of Religions*, ed. Gavin D'Costa (Maryknoll, NY: Orbis, 1990).

36. In Margaret Atwood's novel *The Handmaid's Tale* (London: Virago, 1985), the female narrator, Offred, reflects on how one must make something into an 'it' before killing it: 'That is what you have to do before you kill, I thought. You have to create an it, where none was before. You do that first, in your head, and then you make it real' (p. 202).

37. This basic point has been made in several places by the philosopher Donald Davidson. See, for example, the following quotation: '...a creature that cannot in principle be understood in terms of our own beliefs, values and modes of communication is not a creature that may have thoughts radically different from our own: it is a creature without what we mean by thoughts'. *Expressing Evaluations* (Lawrence, KS: University of Kansas Press, 1984), p. 20. See also 'On the Very Idea of a Conceptual Scheme', reprinted in *Post-Analytic Philosophy*, eds John Rajchman and Cornel West (New York: Columbia University Press, 1985), pp. 129–43.

38. A version of this view is presented by Alasdair MacIntyre in *Whose Justice? Which Rationality?* (London: Duckworth; Notre Dame, IN: University of Notre Dame Press, 1988, chapter 19). For criticisms of MacIntyre's views see Jeffrey Stout's *Ethics After Babel* (Boston: Beacon Press, 1988). For an argument that accepts Stout's views of translation while advocating MacIntyre's position on moral disagreement, see Stephen E. Fowl, 'Could Horace Talk With the Hebrews? Translatability and Moral Disagreement in MacIntyre and Stout', *Journal of Religious Ethics* (forthcoming).

39. See Stout, *Ethics After Babel*, p. 64.

40. ibid., p. 62. While Stout will go on to show that Modernese and Corleone are translatable languages, his point here is slightly misleading. Modernese and Corleone could have absolutely no analogues as far as their moral propositions go and yet still be translatable because of a large degree of overlap in other areas from which analogies could then be drawn to propositions of a moral nature.

41. ibid., pp. 64–5.

42. ibid., p. 65.

# 6

## Living and Dying in the Word:
## Dietrich Bonhoeffer as Performer of Scripture

'This is the Reverend Justus Brake, Provost of the Cathedral, who paid for the Word of God with his life and taught it with his death.'[1] This epitaph was included in a novel that Dietrich Bonhoeffer was writing while he was held in prison during the Second World War. But it is equally appropriate as a description of Bonhoeffer himself.

Throughout his adult life, and even more in the manner of his death, Dietrich Bonhoeffer's guiding concern was with the word of God. That concern was central to his biblical and theological reflection. More importantly, it was central to his own understanding of the relation between Scripture and Christian life. Bonhoeffer sought to discern how people should live in the light of Scripture's witness to Jesus Christ. Indeed, his own life and death represents a powerful example of such discernment.

Thus Bonhoeffer is an important figure for understanding the links between Scripture and Christian ethics. This claim may appear strange to those familiar with Bonhoeffer's life and thought. After all, people have been attracted to the story of Bonhoeffer's life and death. In addition, Bonhoeffer contributed significantly to discussions of such areas as Christology, ecclesiology, ethics, and the relationship between Christian faith and contemporary society. But there has been comparatively little attention paid to Bonhoeffer's scriptural interpretation and its bearing on his understandings of ethics and theology.[2] We think that has more to do with contemporary conceptions of biblical scholarship and of Christian ethics than it has with the strengths and/or weaknesses of Bonhoeffer's readings of Scripture.

In our view, Bonhoeffer was an exemplary performer of Scripture. He powerfully displays the close interrelations between reading and performing Scripture for which we have been arguing in this book. That is not to say that Bonhoeffer's readings of Scripture were completely enacted in his life, or even that his readings are always exemplary.[3] Nor is it to suggest that Bonhoeffer's performance of Scripture is bound to the readings he explicitly offers. In some ways his performance exceeded his readings and thus enabled him to develop better readings of the texts. Nevertheless, Bonhoeffer's life and death exemplify the importance of reading in communion.

It is impossible to summarize Bonhoeffer's life in one chapter. After all, it took Bonhoeffer's close friend and biographer, Eberhard Bethge, more than 800 pages to tell Bonhoeffer's story. Moreover, we do not pretend to describe the complexities of Bonhoeffer's hermeneutical and theological judgements. This chapter is not intended to be either a comprehensive account of Bonhoeffer's biblical exegesis or an evaluation of his theological programme.

Rather, we intend to draw on some of the most significant markers of Bonhoeffer's life and thought in order to show how his reflections on Scripture helped to shape his life, and how the events of his life helped to shape his readings of Scripture.[4] Our discussion is structured around three crucial transitions in Bonhoeffer's life.[5] The first is related to Bonhoeffer's vocational commitment to become a theologian. The second is related to Bonhoeffer's discovery of Scripture and his sense that he had not yet become a Christian. The third is related to Bonhoeffer's involvement in the conspiracy against Hitler.

## LEARNING TO BE A THEOLOGIAN

Dietrich Bonhoeffer was born in 1906 into a comfortable middle-class family. His family was composed primarily of diverse types of professionals. The family was professional, urbane, cultured, and nominally religious.[6] Yet from early on Dietrich announced that he intended to become a theologian. It is unclear exactly why he wanted to do so, and his decision surprised the other members of his family. Ambition, coupled with a presumption that in theology he could have a vocation quite different from other members of his family, almost certainly played important parts in his decision.

Though his family's nominal religiosity kept Dietrich at some distance from the Church, the family was by no means anti-Christian or even non-Christian. There were ministers among Bonhoeffer's more extended family. Moreover, even as a teenager Bonhoeffer took the claims of Christianity increasingly seriously. At the time of his confirmation, Bonhoeffer took to reading Scripture by himself. When he was fifteen he declined to attend a party at a friend's house on the grounds that it was Lent. In school, he began studying Schleiermacher as well as Friedrich Naumann's *Letters on Religion*. The latter's charge that Christianity is little more than an ideal that hovers over the real life of people left a lasting impression on Bonhoeffer. He was unwilling to rest with such a discrepancy between the claims of Christianity and the lives that people led.

In 1923 Bonhoeffer left home to go to university. New worlds opened up to him as he began to expand his studies of philosophy and theology. Even more, a term spent in Rome in 1924 opened up the new world of Roman Catholicism to the Lutheran Bonhoeffer. In Rome, Bonhoeffer wrote, he discovered the Church for the first time.

When he returned to Berlin to the university (1924–7), Bonhoeffer's studies were largely conducted under the guidance of such 'liberal' theologians as Harnack, Holl and Seeberg. They emphasized to Bonhoeffer the importance of scientific theology and historical–critical exegesis of the Bible. During this time, however, Bonhoeffer also became acquainted with the 'dialectical' theology of Karl Barth. Barth's insistence on the centrality of the word of God made a profound impact on Bonhoeffer, and focused his theological musings. In a paper he wrote for Seeberg in 1925, Bonhoeffer challenges the hegemony of a historical interpretation of the Bible. His argument, as Bethge summarizes it, is that 'textual criticism left behind nothing but "dust and ashes"'.... The texts are not just historical sources, but agents of revelation, not just specimens of writing, but sacred canon'. Bonhoeffer insists that readings informed by historical issues are inevitable, because 'none of us can revert to the pre-critical age'. But the importance of that work is relativized: we need interpretation guided by the

Holy Spirit. In Bonhoeffer's terms, 'For history Scripture is only a source, for pneumatology it is testimony.'[7] Such an emphasis on the Spirit and on testimony points to Bonhoeffer's lifelong concern with community, and with understanding the significance of Scripture for Christian life.

By the time he received his doctorate in 1927, Bonhoeffer had proved himself to be such a brilliant student that the faculty saw him as the bright hope for theology. His doctoral dissertation (*Sanctorum Communio* (1927)) and his second thesis (*Act and Being* (1929)) were both significant achievements. They were all the more noteworthy because of Bonhoeffer's relative youth when he wrote them.

Bonhoeffer spent 1928 as an assistant pastor in Barcelona, and then returned to Berlin in 1929–30 as an unpaid lecturer at the university. During this time, Bonhoeffer continued to work on the themes of sociality and community that he had developed in his early writings. He was also busy preaching and teaching in his parish, and lecturing to students in Berlin.

In 1930–1 Bonhoeffer spent a year in America as an exchange student. He went to New York to study at Union Theological Seminary. There, Bonhoeffer developed some friendships that played central roles in his life and thought. A friend he met at the seminary, a black student named Frank Fisher, introduced Bonhoeffer to life in Harlem. Bonhoeffer regularly attended the Abyssinian Baptist Church in Harlem, and he became active in the Sunday school and in various church organizations. Fisher commented on the ease with which Bonhoeffer was accepted by the black community. Perhaps, though Bonhoeffer never indicated as such, he found here the kind of community for which he had been searching in his dissertation.

Another friend whom Bonhoeffer met at the seminary, a French Calvinist named Jean Lasserre, had an important impact on Bonhoeffer's theology. Lasserre was a Christian pacifist. He confronted Bonhoeffer with the force of Jesus' peace commandment. As Bethge characterizes it, Lasserre confronted Bonhoeffer 'with the question of the relationship of the word of God to him as its bearer, as an individual living in the contemporary world'.[8] As a result of Lasserre's influence, Bonhoeffer became much more concerned with issues of peace and their connection to the demands of discipleship. Bonhoeffer became increasingly interested in the relevance of the Sermon on the Mount for Christian life. This interest eventually manifested itself most clearly in his book *The Cost of Discipleship* (1937).

Lasserre helped to transform Bonhoeffer's 'academic knowledge of Lutheran ethics' into a committed identification with Jesus' call to discipleship.[9] The change was significant. For example, during his time in Barcelona in 1928 Bonhoeffer had written, 'For what I have I thank [Germany], through this nation I became what I am.'[10] During his time in New York in 1930–1, as a result both of nationalist developments in Germany and his friendships with people like Fisher and Lasserre, Bonhoeffer's position had changed:

> You have brothers and sisters in our people and in every people; do not forget that. Whatever may happen, let us never again forget that the people of God are one Christian people, that no nationalism, no race or class hatred, can strike effective blows if we are one.[11]

The time in America helped to set the stage for a crucial transition in Bonhoeffer's life that occurred after he returned to Germany in 1931.

## DISCOVERING SCRIPTURE AND BECOMING A CHRISTIAN

When Bonhoeffer returned to Germany, he assumed a position as a lecturer in the theological faculty of Berlin University. He also became involved in ecumenical work. Perhaps most importantly, however, Bonhoeffer experienced some decisive changes in his own life and thought. Bonhoeffer spent more and more time meditating on Scripture. He focused on the Sermon on the Mount not merely as a source for understanding, but as a word to be acted upon.

In a letter to his girlfriend, Maria von Wedemeyer, in 1936, Bonhoeffer reflected on the changes in his life during 1931–2:

> I plunged into work in a very unchristian way. An...ambition that many noticed in me made my life difficult...
>    Then something happened, something that has changed and transformed my life to the present day. For the first time I discovered the Bible...I had often preached, I had seen a great deal of the Church,

and talked and preached about it – but I had not yet become a Christian...

I know that at that time I turned the doctrine of Jesus Christ into something of personal advantage for myself...I pray to God that that will never happen again. Also I had never prayed, or prayed only very little. For all my loneliness, I was quite pleased with myself. Then the Bible, and in particular the Sermon on the Mount, freed me from that. Since then everything has changed. I have felt this plainly, and so have other people about me. It was a great liberation. It became clear to me that the life of a servant of Jesus Christ must belong to the Church, and step by step it became plainer to me how far that must go.[12]

In Bonhoeffer's own judgement, prior to 1931–2 he had been a theologian who had not yet become a Christian. What makes the difference? In large measure, the difference lies in his view that he now discovered Scripture 'for the first time'.

Bonhoeffer was not suggesting that he simply began to read Scripture, for he had been doing that since his confirmation days. Moreover, he had engaged in various studies of Scripture and methods of biblical interpretation during his days as a student and lecturer, and he had led Bible studies and preached while serving as a pastor in Barcelona.

Bonhoeffer's point was that previously he had read the Bible *for* himself, but now he discovered the importance of reading Scripture *over-against* himself. In August of 1932, during a youth conference, Bonhoeffer observed:

Has it not become terrifyingly clear again and again, in everything that we have said here to one another, that we are no longer obedient to the Bible? We are more fond of our own thoughts than of the thoughts of the Bible. We no longer read the Bible seriously, we no longer read it against ourselves, but for ourselves. If the whole of our conference here is to have any great significance, it may be perhaps that of showing us that we must read the Bible in quite a different way, until we find ourselves again.[13]

From this time on, Bonhoeffer's life and thought are formed around this conviction that we must learn to read Scripture 'in quite a different way'.[14] Until this time, Bonhoeffer's reading of Scripture was informed by a reading of the world into which he had been inculturated as both a Lutheran and a German. However, Bonhoeffer came to question parts of this reading of the world on the basis of his experiences abroad and his reading of Scripture. Consequently, he discovered the importance

of allowing Scripture to challenge the presumptions with which we
come to the text.

Bonhoeffer began to see more clearly that seeing the Bible as a
'source' meant that we could simply read the Bible for ourselves.
Reading it pneumatologically, however, and seeing Scripture as
'testimony', meant that we would need to read Scripture over-
against ourselves.

During the winter term of 1932–3 at the University of Berlin,
Bonhoeffer began to take some tentative steps towards reading
Scripture against himself in a series of lectures he gave on
Genesis 1–3. The lectures were designed to provide a theological
interpretation of the scriptural texts, as he indicated in the
Introduction that he wrote when the lectures were published:

> The Bible is nothing but the book upon which the Church stands. This
> is its essential nature, or it is nothing. Therefore the Scriptures need to
> be read and proclaimed wholly from the viewpoint of the end. Thus
> the creation story should be read in church in the first place only from
> Christ, and not until then as leading to Christ. We can read towards
> Christ only if we know that Christ is the beginning, the new and the
> end of our world.
> Theological interpretation accepts the Bible as the book of the
> Church and interprets it as such. Its method is this assumption; it
> continually refers back from the text (which has to be ascertained
> with all the methods of philological and historical research) to this
> supposition.[15]

Bonhoeffer's insistence on a theological interpretation of Scripture
shows the continuity of his concerns from his studies with Seeberg.
Bonhoeffer notes the importance of taking into account philological
and historical research, but a theological reading is primary.

Moreover, Bonhoeffer emphasizes the importance of reading
Scripture over-against ourselves. When he wrote the new Introduction in 1933, Hitler was already on the rise. Thus Bonhoeffer's
eschatological emphasis has political significance:

> The Church of Christ bears witness to the end of all things. It lives from
> the end, it thinks from the end, it acts from the end, it proclaims its
> message from the end.... But the Church is naturally in tumult when
> these children of the world that has passed away lay claim to the Church,
> to the new, for themselves. They want the new and only know the old.
> And thus they deny Christ the Lord.[16]

Unfortunately, Bonhoeffer's interpretation was not particularly
well received in academic circles. As Bethge characterizes it,

'The exegetists regarded it as systematics and the systematicians regareded it as exegesis. The former were indignant and the latter took no notice.'[17]

Bonhoeffer's theological challenge to Hitler soon became more explicit. In 1933, as Hitler was coming to power, Bonhoeffer delivered a series of lectures on Christology. He insisted that Jesus Christ, the *risen* Christ, is present in the word, in the sacrament, and in the community. The lectures represented a challenge not only to the reigning liberal theology, but also to the emerging pretensions of Hitler. Moreover, Bonhoeffer's first sermon after Hitler's accession to power dealt with Gideon, the champion of God, who at God's direction attacked and conquered with an absurdly small force.[18]

Such a sermon was appropriate, for indeed the number of Christians who recognized Hitler's threat was absurdly small. The vast majority of Christians swore allegiance to Hitler, forming what became known as the German Christian Church. Bonhoeffer perceived this as a threat to the Church and to the Lordship of Christ, and in July 1933 he preached a sermon on the rock against which the gates of hell shall not prevail:

...it will not be taken from us – its name is decision, its name is discerning of the spirits.... Come...you who have been left alone, you who have lost the Church, let us return to Holy Writ, let us go forth and seek the Church together.... For the times, which are times of collapse to the human understanding may well be for her a great time of building.... Church, remain a church!.... Confess, confess, confess.[19]

Bonhoeffer preached, lectured and distributed pamphlets; he helped to form – along with his friend Martin Niemöller – a 'Pastors Emergency League' to deal with the threat. But these activities did not make an appreciable difference. In the autumn of 1933, Bonhoeffer told a group of his students that 'We must now endure in silence, and set the firebrand of truth to all four corners of the proud German Christian edifice so that one day the whole structure may collapse.'[20] And so, as part of that endurance, in October 1933 Bonhoeffer accepted a call to pastor a German congregation in England. During the next two years he would watch and think about how to deal with the gathering storm in Germany.

During his time in England, Bonhoeffer struggled to discern the word of the Lord in the midst of the emerging troubles in Germany and beyond. Those struggles led him to return to the Sermon on the Mount. In a letter to a friend in 1934, he asked for help in knowing how to preach on those texts, noting that the Sermon on the Mount 'always comes back to *keeping* the commandment and not evading it. Discipleship of Christ – I'd like to know what that is – it is not exhausted in our concept of faith.'[21] Bonhoeffer also found himself returning to the mission of a reluctant yet obedient Jeremiah as a model for his own life.[22]

Bonhoeffer's time in England renewed a long-standing interest he had in visiting India. As he perceived the West to be disintegrating, he had wanted to see if there might be something to the convictions held and the questions addressed in the East. Bonhoeffer even indicated that it sometimes seemed as if 'there's more Christianity in their "paganism" than in the whole of our Reich Church'.[23] But he also wanted to go to India to become acquainted with Gandhi's understanding of non-violence and community. Bonhoeffer thought that Gandhi might help him understand how the Confessing Church[24] could resist Hitler, while also being obedient to the Sermon on the Mount.

But rather than going to India, circumstances led him to return to Germany in 1935. Bonhoeffer returned to become a pastor-in-charge of a seminary newly founded by the Confessing Church, eventually located at Finkenwalde. Here Bonhoeffer was given the task of preparing clergy to serve churches that would be able to resist the claims of Hitler. In Bonhoeffer's view, that required a revitalization of discipleship learned and lived in Christian community. As he wrote to his brother in 1935:

> The restoration of the Church must surely depend on a new kind of monasticism, having nothing in common with the old but a life of uncompromising adherence to the Sermon on the Mount in imitation of Christ. I believe the time has come to rally men together for this.[25]

Hence Bonhoeffer's seminary was established not simply as a place to learn about the Bible and the history of the Church, nor even a place to acquire the techniques of running a parish. Neither was it to foster a monasticism that existed in isolation from the world, though it did involve a 'turning' from the 'world'.[26] As Bonhoeffer described it, 'The aim is not the seclusion of the monastery, but a place of the deepest inward concentration for service outside.'[27] Thus Bonhoeffer's seminary was to be a place where the students would be initiated into a way of life, structured around the sacraments, Scripture, and communal discipline that would enable them to serve in the world.

Indeed, in Bonhoeffer's view, the primary task of the seminary was to help the students learn how to pray and how to read Scripture. The Finkenwalde community set aside time each day for prayer and for meditating on Scripture. That struck some people, even within the Confessing Church, as an odd way to run a seminary. Even worse, it seemed to be too focused on rules and outward appearances. But Bonhoeffer rejected such a view. In a letter to Karl Barth in 1936, Bonhoeffer wrote that:

> [The need to pray] is not obviated, even by the Confessing Church.... The imputation that these [i.e. periods of meditation and prayer] are legalistic, strikes me as totally unreal. How can it possibly be legalistic for a Christian to learn what prayer is, and to spend a fair amount of his time learning it? Recently a leading member of the Confessing Church told me: 'We haven't the time for meditation now; the ordinands must learn to preach and to catechize.' This either shows a total incomprehension of young theologians today, or else a blasphemous ignorance of how preaching and teaching come about. The kind of questions serious young theologians put to us are: How can I learn to pray? How can I learn to read the Bible? Either we can help them to do this, or we can't help them at all. Nothing of all this can be taken for granted.[28]

The most important activities of the community at Finkenwalde were those practices in which people learned to pray and to read Scripture. Even the practice of solitary meditation every morning was understood to be a part of communal living.[29]

For Bonhoeffer, Christian community is essential because it is in and through such community that we are formed to read Scripture wisely and to live as Christians in the world. But Bonhoeffer also knew that to talk about reading Scripture in community raised questions not only of biblical interpretation, but also of ethics and politics.[30] The German Christians were reading the Bible at the same time as the Confessing Church, but they were coming to vastly different conclusions about how a Christian ought to live. What was the difference?

Bonhoeffer addressed that question in a lecture to the Confessing Church entitled 'The Presentation of New Testament Texts'. At the outset he distinguishes two different ways of understanding the title phrase:

The phrase means either that the biblical message must justify itself to the present age and in that way must show itself capable of being made present, or that the present age must justify itself before the biblical message and in that way the message must become present.[31]

The German Christians, in continuity with much of the theology that had been written since the Enlightenment, followed the first path. This requires that the Bible be sifted through the sieve of humanity's own current views and desires. What does not go through is scorned and tossed away as a vestige of an antiquated and primitive culture. This path tends to make the question of method central, and thereby evades the question of content.[32]

In direct contrast, the second path makes the question of content central. The present age must justify itself before the content of the biblical message. If we want to be most 'relevant' in the 'present', Bonhoeffer argues, then we ought to immerse ourselves in Scripture:

> *The present* is not where the present age announces its claim before Christ, but where the present age stands before the claims of Christ, for the concept of the present is determined not by a temporal definition but by the Word of Christ as the Word of God.[33]

In Bonhoeffer's view, the presentation of the gospel is best achieved not through methodological principles or through the attempt to make Scripture 'relevant'. It is achieved when people are willing to learn to allow the present age in general, and our lives in particular, to be interrogated by the Scriptures. The German Christians only read the Bible *for* themselves, discarding what they didn't want. But the call is to read Scripture *over-against* ourselves, allowing Scripture to question our lives.

During this same period, Bonhoeffer also engaged in substantial study of, and lecturing on, texts from the Old Testament. Three lectures in particular in 1935-6, 'Christ in the Psalms', 'King David', and 'The Reconstruction of Jerusalem According to Ezra and Nehemiah', provide important indications of Bonhoeffer's readings of Scripture in relation to his life.[34] In these lectures Bonhoeffer emphasizes a christological reading of the Old Testament. That in itself should not be surprising, for Bonhoeffer understood all of Scripture to be the book of Christ. Bonhoeffer read these texts not simply as past events in the life of Israel, but more particularly in relation to the light of Christ and the continuing life of the Church. As Martin Kuske has argued in reference to 'King David', Bonhoeffer.

> led, so to speak, a discussion between three partners: the church in which he lived, the crucified Lord, and the David stories. The church can enter into the discussion with these stories only by way of and through the mediation of Christ, but they also have something important to say to the church: God judges his church in the present with the goal of renewal.[35]

In all three lectures, Bonhoeffer's readings of the Old Testament serve not simply to endorse the Church, but also to challenge it. He employs textual and literary-criticism where it is useful, but his primary focus is theological.

Even so, Bonhoeffer's Christological method and the content of these lectures have received considerable criticism from Old Testament scholars, both at the time Bonhoeffer gave them and in more recent years.[36] Some of the criticisms are well-taken, particularly in relation to such specific exegetical issues as whether Bonhoeffer's reading of Ezra takes adequate account of verses that challenge his argument.[37] But the criticisms also reflect presumptions that give hegemony to historical–critical exegesis and thereby deem other readings, including those that are Christological and/or those concerned not simply with the past but with action in the present, as somehow deficient.[38]

Such criticisms also miss the importance of Bonhoeffer's readings of the Old Testament in relation to other options in Germany. In contrast to attacks on the Old Testament by both German Christians and by National Socialists,[39] Bonhoeffer insisted on the importance of the Old Testament for Christians.[40] Bonhoeffer had argued as early as his lectures on Genesis 1–3 that God is the *One* God in the whole of Scripture. He returns to that point in a note to the study 'King David', where he contended that 'The God of the Old Testament is the Father of Jesus Christ. The God who appears in Jesus Christ is the God of the Old Testament. He is the triune God.'[41] The Old Testament cannot be dispensed with as a more 'primitive' stage in the development of religion, nor can the Jews be dispensed with simply as precursors to the Christians. The God of Israel is also the God of Jesus Christ. Bonhoeffer's developing sense of the importance of the Old Testament for Christians was thus an important means of resisting the idolatrous claims of the Nazis and the German Christians who supported them.

In Finkenwalde, Bonhoeffer sought to develop a Christian community whose practices would be structured so that the community members' lives would be located in the Scriptures. Bonhoeffer's instructions on meditation to the seminarians reminded them that 'grounded in the Scripture, we learn to speak to God in the language which God has spoken to us'.[42] Becoming a disciple of Jesus Christ required nothing less.

These convictions form the core of Bonhoeffer's famous books, *The Cost of Discipleship* and *Life Together*, both written during the time of the Finkenwalde seminary. In *The Cost of Discipleship* a number of Bonhoeffer's long-standing concerns, including his focus on the Sermon on the Mount, receive sustained treatment. First, Bonhoeffer insists that the life of discipleship requires a costly commitment to following the way of the Crucified One. He undertakes a polemic against 'cheap grace'. When grace is cheap, the Christian life

> comes to mean nothing more than living in the world and as the world, in being no different from the world, in fact, in being prohibited from being different from the world for the sake of grace. The upshot of it all is that my only duty as a Christian is to leave the world for an hour or so on a Sunday morning and go to church to be assured that my sins are all forgiven.

In direct contrast, Bonhoeffer contends that the only person 'who has the right to say that he is justified by grace alone is the [one] who has left all to follow Christ'.[43] Bonhoeffer's polemic against cheap grace, rather obviously directed (at least in the first instance) towards the German Christians, is analogous to his argument against reading the Bible in order to justify the present age. In both instances, the result is that people remain of the 'world' and are unable to live as disciples of Jesus Christ.

Second, Bonhoeffer's concern with sociality and community is prominent. Here, however, his concern is not so much with a philosophy of sociality as it is with the particular eucharistic community called into being by the God of Jesus Christ. Bonhoeffer shows how such a community, patterned in Scripture, entails a discipline of caring for one another, reproving one another, guiding one another. He argues that discipleship in community requires practices of forgiveness and reconciliation, including confession of sins as preparation for the Eucharist. Such a community also entails, as *The Cost of Discipleship* not only argues but manifests, that we learn to read Scripture not only for ourselves but over-against ourselves.

Moreover, Bonhoeffer insists on a sharp distinction between the Church and the world. Drawing on biblical texts as diverse as Genesis 6.14 (the story of Noah's Ark), Ephesians 1.13ff. and 4.30, 1 Thessalonians 5.23, and 1 Peter 1.5, Bonhoeffer argues that 'The community of the saints is barred off from the world by an unbreakable seal, awaiting its ultimate deliverance. Like a sealed train travelling through foreign territory, the Church goes on its way through the world.'[44] As such, sanctification is possible only in the Church.

Even so, Bonhoeffer also argues that Christians cannot withdraw into a spiritual inwardness that fails to confront the world's opposition. While Christians are not to be of the world, we are to confront the world:

> Now the Church is the city set on the hill and founded on earth by the direct act of God, it is the *'polis'* of Matt. 5:14, and as such it is God's own sealed possession. Hence there is a certain 'political' character involved in the idea of sanctification and it is this character which provides the only basis for the Church's political ethic. The world is the world and the Church is the Church, and yet the Word of God must go forth from the Church into all the world, proclaiming that the earth is the Lord's and all that therein is. Herein lies the 'political' character of the Church.[45]

In the midst of Nazi Germany, Bonhoeffer insisted that only a Christian community that is immersed in Scripture and is willing to confront the idolatrous claims of Nazism by serving in the world is capable of an authentic politics.

A third emphasis in *The Cost of Discipleship* is Bonhoeffer's claim that Christians should *not* resist evil. He argues that 'evil becomes a spent force when we put up no resistance'. Suffering that is willingly endured is stronger than evil. Such suffering takes its form in the Church of the crucified Christ, and so the vocation of the Christian community is to be willing to suffer for the sake of the world. Bonhoeffer argues that 'there is no deed on earth so outrageous as to justify a different attitude. The worse the evil, the readier must the Christian be to suffer; he must let the evil person fall into Jesus' hands.'[46]

Even so, a few short pages later in *The Cost of Discipleship*, Bonhoeffer also contends that 'to make non-resistance a principle for secular life is to deny God, by undermining his gracious ordinance for the preservation of the world'.[47] Here Bonhoeffer seems to point in the direction that leads to his fateful decision to join in a plot to assassinate Hitler. Does Bonhoeffer come to the conclusion that Scripture in general, and the Sermon on the Mount in particular, simply aren't practical in the modern secular world and thus ought to be abandoned? Is this where Bonhoeffer the exemplary performer of Scripture ends, and a different kind of character emerges?

Was Bonhoeffer's decision to join the resistance to Hitler a decisive mistake and an abandonment of his Christian convictions? Alternatively, was his decision appropriate and thus morally praiseworthy? In our view both ways of framing the question oversimplify the issues. While there were some important shifts in Bonhoeffer's thought as well as his life, those shifts reflect a greater continuity than is sometimes assumed.

As we will show, it is *not* the case that Bonhoeffer the Christian became Bonhoeffer the worldly humanist who recognized that the 'real' world is the world of politics and statecraft and war. Rather, the readings of Scripture of Bonhoeffer the Christian were interrelated in complex ways with his readings of the world.

## READING THE WORLD AND CHRIST IN THE WORLD

As we have already argued, Bonhoeffer's time of discovering Scripture and learning to become a Christian was also a time of activity and engagement in the world. Even so, there was another transition in Bonhoeffer's life, and this one happened during 1939 and 1940. His life and thought became more focused on the world. Increasingly, Bonhoeffer's reading of the world alters his reading of Scripture.

A number of significant events between 1937 and 1940 occasioned this shift. Finkenwalde was shut down in 1937. By 1940 all of the Confessing Church's seminaries had been closed down by the Gestapo. The Confessing Church itself was also falling apart. Most of Bonhoeffer's seminarians from Finkenwalde had been called into military service. The Nazis had effectively dismantled the community that provided the backdrop for *The*

*Cost of Discipleship.*

In November 1938, the Nazis unleashed a reign of terror against the Jewish population. It became known as the 'Crystal Night'. A few days after this event, Bonhoeffer sent a circular to the dispersed Finkenwaldians in which he wrote: 'I have lately been thinking a great deal about Psalm 74, Zech. 2:8 and Rom. 9:4f. and 11:11–15. That leads us into very earnest prayer.' It may have also been at this time that Bonhoeffer produced the dictum that he impressed upon students: 'Only he who cries out for the Jews may sing Gregorian chants.'[48] Bonhoeffer had long been concerned with the treatment of the Jews, but now he began to see the urgency of action in a clearer light.[49]

In 1939 Bonhoeffer returned to England for two months, and to America for what was to be a year. He made these journeys at least in part in order to avoid military service. In a letter to Bishop Bell of England, a long-time friend and confidant, Bonhoeffer reflected on the difficulties of accepting military service:

I am thinking of leaving Germany sometime. The main reason is the compulsory military service to which the men of my age (1906) will be called up this year. It seems to me conscientiously impossible to join in a war under the present circumstances. On the other hand the Confessional [sic] Church as such has not taken any definite attitude in this respect and probably cannot take it as things are. So I should cause a tremendous damage to my brethren if I would make a stand on this point which would be regarded by the regime as typical of the hostility of our Church towards the State. Perhaps the worst thing of all is the military oath which I should have to swear. So I am rather puzzled in this situation, and perhaps even more because I feel it is really only on Christian grounds that I find it difficult to do military service under the present conditions, *and yet there are only very few friends who would approve of my attitude.*[50]

Bonhoeffer perceived a lack of Christian community that would help him both to discern the path he ought to take and to sustain him in taking it. While the Confessing Church had not completely collapsed by this point, it was largely unable to form and sustain disciples who could discern how best to respond to the Nazis.

Shortly after he arrived in America, however, Bonhoeffer decided to return to Germany. Bonhoeffer wrote a letter to Reinhold Niebuhr in which he outlined the reasons for his decision:

I have made a mistake in coming to America. I must live through this difficult period of our national history with the Christian people of Germany. I will have no right to participate in the reconstruction of Christian life in Germany after the war if I do not share the trials of this time with my people...Christians in Germany will face the terrible alternative of either willing the defeat of their nation in order that Christian civilization may survive, or willing the victory of their nation and thereby destroying our civilization. I know which of these alternatives I must choose; but I cannot make that choice in security.[51]

Bonhoeffer's return to Germany reflected his willingness to bear responsibility and accept guilt for his church, his nation and his class.[52]

Thus Bonhoeffer returned in 1939 to a Germany where Christian community had largely been eclipsed by the Nazis, where the cries of the Jews needed to be heard, and where he believed he needed to bear responsibility for what was happening in Germany. It was in this context that Bonhoeffer went to work for the *Abwehr*, the German army's counter-intelligence outfit. He became a spy, and thereby he could remain in Germany without having to become an actual soldier in the military. But Bonhoeffer was more than a spy for the *Abwehr*; he was a double-agent who assisted Jews in escaping Germany, let the Allies know of events developing in Germany, and engaged in an ill-fated plot to assassinate Hitler. Bonhoeffer had always been involved in the world; but by 1940 he had become intensely and intimately involved with the issues of his contemporary world, his place, and his time.

During the years 1940–3, while working as a double-agent, Bonhoeffer sketched a number of fragments for a book on ethics that he thought would be his life work. Unfortunately, he would never be able to complete the *Ethics*.[53] In 1943 Bonhoeffer was arrested by the Gestapo and imprisoned for questioning. Initially, his arrest was for his assistance to the Jews. It was only later, after the plot to assassinate Hitler failed in July 1944, that Bonhoeffer himself was implicated in the resistance to Hitler. In prison, Bonhoeffer kept up a clandestine yet vigorous correspondence with various people, particularly his close friend and former Finkenwalde student, Eberhard Bethge. That correspondence contains Bonhoeffer's last theological reflections, later edited and published by Bethge. Bonhoeffer remained in prison until 9 April 1945, when he was hanged by the Nazis as a traitor.

The eclipse of Christian community, the cries of the Jews, and the guilt and responsibility that Bonhoeffer felt belonged to his

Church, his nation and his class form the context that shapes the final years of Bonhoeffer's life. Within this context it seems that the twists and turns of this decisive period in Bonhoeffer's life and death are more dependent on his reading of the world than on his readings of Scripture. Clearly, these developments affect Bonhoeffer's reading of Scripture. One of our contentions, however, is that in spite of the tumultuous nature of Bonhoeffer's final years, events in the world never displace his reading of Scripture. It is important to trace some of the developments of his thought before returning to the question of the relations between his readings of Scripture and his decision to participate in the resistance to Hitler.

Bonhoeffer came to believe that he needed to risk his life for the sake of others and for the sake of a better future for the Church, the nation and the world. Bonhoeffer had argued in *The Cost of Discipleship* that the Church must be willing to suffer, but the tendency in that book was to make a sharp distinction between the Church's suffering and the world's. Even here, however, in a reflection on Matthew 5.10, Bonhoeffer argued that 'Jesus gives his blessing not merely to suffering incurred directly for the confession of his name, but to suffering in any just cause.'[54]

That conviction becomes even more prominent in *Ethics*.[55] Through the Confessing Church's recognition of making a stand against the German Christians, Bonhoeffer had come to see the importance of the exclusive claim of Christ as reflected in Matthew 12.30: 'He that is not with me is against me.' But Bonhoeffer also came to recognize that there were non-Christians whose resistance to Hitler and whose commitments to endangered values brought them very close to a Christian standpoint. In this light, Bonhoeffer turned to Mark 9.40: 'He that is not against us is for us.'

Bonhoeffer argued that both passages are crucial for an adequate understanding of the claims of Jesus Christ on Christian life:

These two sayings [Matthew 12.30 and Mark 9.40] necessarily belong together as the two claims of Jesus Christ, the claim to exclusiveness and the claim to totality. The greater the exclusiveness, the greater the freedom. But in isolation the claim to exclusiveness leads to fanaticism and to slavery; and in isolation the claim to totality leads to the secularization and self-abandonment of the Church. The more exclusively we acknowledge and confess Christ as our Lord, the more fully the wide range of His dominion will be disclosed to us.[56]

Christ's claim to exclusiveness had been a theme prominent in
*The Cost of Discipleship*. Christ's claim to totality (which is, for
Bonhoeffer, quite different from the Nazis 'totalizing' claims)
emerges as a theme in relation to Bonhoeffer's involvement in
the resistance and his reading of Mark 9.40. It also becomes
a prominent focus of both *Ethics* and *Letters and Papers from
Prison*.[57]

Bonhoeffer's focus on 'the wide range of His dominion' in
his later work also led him to revise some of his earlier views,
particularly his sharp distinctions between the Church and the
world in *The Cost of Discipleship*. No longer is the Church 'like
a sealed train travelling through foreign territory' as it goes its
way in the world. In *Ethics*, Christ's claim to totality means that
the world is not foreign territory; it is where Christ is found. The
Church may be foreign to the world, but that is only by virtue of
the testimony that it bears. The reality of God disclosed in Jesus
Christ belongs not to the Church, but to the world.[58]

Indeed Bonhoeffer drew on such passages as Colossians 1.15ff.
in developing what Larry Rasmussen has aptly characterized as
a 'christocratic understanding of all reality'.[59] Thus we must
move away from 'thinking in terms of two spheres', Bonhoeffer
argued, and recognize that there is only one reality – 'the reality
of God, which has become manifest in Christ in the reality of
the world'.[60] But the reality of the world is not self-evident. It
requires an ability to discern the ever-changing manner in which
Christ takes form in the world. Bonhoeffer argued that 'the New
Testament is concerned solely with the manner in which the reality
of Christ assumes reality in the present world, which it has already
encompassed, seized, and possessed'.[61]

Thus the pivotal question for Bonhoeffer becomes 'Who is
Christ for us today?'[62] The question presumes that there is no
once-and-for-all answer. The form of Christ must be apprehended
anew in each and every historical situation. As Bonhoeffer puts
it, 'What can and must be said is not what is good once and for
all, but the way in which Christ takes form among us here and
now.'[63] But such a claim needs further unpacking: what does he
mean by 'Christ', who is the 'us', and how should we understand
the 'here and now'?

In Bonhoeffer's view, the form of Jesus Christ is discovered through his incarnation, his crucifixion and his resurrection.[64] Christian life must embrace the entire scope of Christ's life, as the following extended quotation from *Ethics* illustrates:

> In Jesus Christ we have faith in the incarnate, crucified and risen God. In the incarnation we learn of the love of God for His creation; in the crucifixion we learn of the judgement of God upon all flesh; and in the resurrection we learn of God's will for a new world. There could be no greater error than to tear these three elements apart; for each of them comprises the whole. It is quite wrong to establish a separate theology of the incarnation, a theology of the cross, or a theology of the resurrection, each in opposition to the others, by a misconceived absolutization of one of these parts; it is equally wrong to apply the same procedure to a consideration of the Christian life. A Christian ethic constructed solely on the basis of the incarnation would lead directly to the compromise solution. An ethic which was based solely on the cross or the resurrection of Jesus would fall victim to radicalism and enthusiasm. Only in the unity is the conflict resolved.[65]

Christian life receives its form and unity in the interplay of the incarnation, crucifixion and resurrection. As Rasmussen has instructively characterized Bonhoeffer's view, the unity of a Christian's action 'lies in conforming to the [form of Christ] in the given time and place and finding the fitting response there (*sachgemäss*); that is, determining whether the conforming action is one of "incarnation" (affirmation and co-operation), "crucifixion" (judgement and rejection) or "resurrection" (bold creativity and newness)'.[66]

Thus as Christ's life has a polyphonic character, so also does the Christian's. In one of his letters to Eberhard Bethge, Bonhoeffer referred to the 'polyphony of life', and then asked: 'May not the attraction and importance of polyphony in music consist in its being a musical reflection of this Christological fact [the divine and human nature] and therefore of our *vita christiana*?'[67] In a letter dated 21 July 1944, the day after the plot against Hitler failed, Bonhoeffer concluded that we must learn to live completely in this world. By that he did not mean to suggest the 'shallow and banal this-worldliness of the enlightened, the busy, the comfortable, or the lascivious, but the profound this-worldliness, characterized by discipline and the constant knowledge of death and resurrection'. In the midst of that profound this-worldliness, Bonhoeffer argued, we need to live 'unreservedly in life's duties, problems, successes and failures, experiences and perplexities'.[68]

Even so, one might ask who is the 'we' who are to live unreservedly in life's duties and who is the 'us' whom Christ is for today? On the one hand, it would seem that the reference is all-encompassing. Because Christ is the form of the world, the claim is addressed to all people – Christian and non-Christian – alike. But that would seem to subvert any notion of a particularistic Christian identity, and Bonhoeffer thought that 'righteous action' alone could not be sustained very long.

Thus on the other hand, Bonhoeffer wanted to preserve a sense of 'us' that refers specifically to Christian identity. He rejected a sharp distinction between the Church and the world, but he also did not want the Church simply to become the world. In the *Letters and Papers from Prison*, Bonhoeffer briefly adverts to the importance of an 'arcane discipline' (or 'discipline of the secret') whose purpose would be to carve out a space for the formation and sustenance of Christian identity and the protection of the mysteries of the faith.[69] The notion of such a discipline refers historically to the ancient practice of the Church whereby only the baptized were allowed to be present for the Eucharist. In this way, the mysteries of the faith were preserved from profanation.

For Bonhoeffer, the purpose of such a discipline in contemporary life is not a withdrawal from the world or some kind of secret enclave in isolation from the world. Bonhoeffer did not want to revert to 'thinking in terms of two spheres'. The Church is to stand 'in the middle of the village', not on the boundaries; it is to be a Church for others.[70] Thus the aim of the discipline of the secret is to provide the space for formation and discernment to enable appropriate service in the world. It is in such a discipline that Scripture would be read and proclaimed and the sacraments celebrated, where people would learn to pray and worship for the sake of the world.

The basic thread of Bonhoeffer's argument for the 'discipline of the secret' can be found earlier, in his practical attempts at the formation and sustenance of a Christian community that would recover the insights of monasticism while being of service in the world. Despite the difference between *The Cost of Discipleship* and his later work in the characterization of the relations between the Church and the world, Bonhoeffer's discussion of the 'discipline of the secret' shows the continuity of his emphasis on carving out spaces where people can learn to become performers of Scripture.

The discipline of the secret is also important in Bonhoeffer's thought as a space where Christians can develop the habits and skills needed to discern who Christ is 'today', to articulate how Christ is taking form among us 'here and now'.[71] Such discernment requires learning to read Scripture in communion with others in the Body of Christ, fully recognizing the polyphonic character of the Christ who is the centre of Scripture.

Moreover, the emphasis on the 'today' and the 'here and now' is a reminder that we also need accurate readings of the world, something Bonhoeffer had recognized as early as 1932:

...The word of the church to the world must...encounter the world in all its present reality from the deepest knowledge of the world, if it is to be authoritative. Out of this knowledge the church must here and now be able to speak the Word of God, the word of authority in the most concrete way.... To us God is 'always' God 'today'.[72]

Hence the discernment of how Christians ought to live involves learning to engage powerful readings both of Scripture and also of the world. It is only in this way, according to Bonhoeffer, that we can adequately answer the question 'who Christ is for us today'.

For Bonhoeffer, we ought not to engage readings both of Scripture and of the world without recovering the centrality of the Old Testament. This is so in several ways. First, the Old Testament is important for understanding the significance of Jesus Christ, and Bonhoeffer came to believe that the Old Testament ought to be read in relation to the various marks of Christ's life.[73] Bonhoeffer's Christological reading of the Old Testament, however, does not reduce the Old Testament to an allegorical code that loses any independent significance. So whereas he often read the Psalms in relation to the crucified Christ (particularly Psalm 58), Bonhoeffer also suggested in a letter to Bethge that the Song of Songs should be read incarnationally, arguing that the 'best "Christological" exposition' of it is to read it as an ordinary love song.[74]

Moreover, whereas in the mid-1930s Bonhoeffer had emphasized the importance of reading the Old Testament in the light of the New, in *Letters and Papers from Prison* Bonhoeffer argued that 'we still read the New Testament far too little in the light of the Old'.[75] Indeed Kuske argues that Bonhoeffer's complex and controversial comments on godlessness and 'the world come of age' are closely tied not only to Christ's crucifixion, but also to his reading of the Old Testament prophets of judgement. They proclaimed the extent to which a powerless God is powerful.[76]

Bonhoeffer was convinced that the Old Testament is central for a wise discernment of who Christ is for us today. But that also returns us to the question of Bonhoeffer's participation in the resistance and its relation to his readings of Scripture.

## CONCLUSION: BONHOEFFER AS PERFORMER OF SCRIPTURE

While he was in prison, Bonhoeffer became increasingly interested in the Old Testament stories of people who, as he put it, did such things as lie, kill, and deceive – and often to the glory of God! Through his own co-operation with the resistance, Bonhoeffer was forced to lie and he was ready to kill. Thus it is perhaps not surprising that Bonhoeffer refused to consign these Old Testament texts to an 'earlier stage' of religion, contending that it is one and the same God.[77]

To be sure, Bonhoeffer did not actually turn to those stories as an attempt to give reasons for his actions, nor does he actually give readings of the texts themselves. Even so, it would appear that this is a case where Bonhoeffer reads Scripture more for himself and less over-against himself. Simply to turn to these stories in the Old Testament without reference to the New Testament texts or to Jesus Christ would appear to be a questionable reading strategy. Even if it is the case, as we think it is, that Bonhoeffer is right in saying that we do not often enough read the New Testament in the light of the Old, the point is still that we need to see the two in relation to each other.

But perhaps it would be more fair simply to recognize that Bonhoeffer was searching for an adequate understanding both of Scripture and the world in a context of extremity. The isolated prison cell in Tegel was a long way from the community of Finkenwalde. And it would be consistent with Bonhoeffer's own convictions to suggest that we are less likely to read Scripture wisely when we do so outside the context of Christian community.

Indeed, the lack of a particular Christian community influenced the course of events from Bonhoeffer's decision to join the resistance all the way up to his death, including his readings of Scripture and his readings of the world. Bonhoeffer ended up relying not on the shared friendships and practices of Christian community to form his judgements, but on the practices and skills of his cohorts in the resistance and in his family. Bonhoeffer's letter to Bishop Bell (cited above), in which he laments the lack of friends who share his convictions, undoubtedly reflects a situation in which the continuing existence of a Christian community like that described in *Life Together* and *The Cost of Discipleship* might have made a significant difference.

Bonhoeffer knew that his decision to join the resistance might require that he give up his life. When he was asked about the passage in the New Testament that 'all who take the sword will perish by the sword' (Matt. 26.52), Bonhoeffer replied that the word was valid for those in the resistance as well. They too were subject to the judgement, but the time was such that people were needed who would accept the risk.[78]

Bonhoeffer understood his participation in the resistance as an act of repentance for the guilt of his Church, his nation, and also his class.[79] Because his Church, his nation and his class were all complicit in helping to give rise to Hitler, they needed to act. But he also knew that there would be punishment by God. Thus by taking up the sword, Bonhoeffer also presumed that he would need to 'pray to God for the forgiveness of the sin and pray for peace'.[80]

It would appear that, had the Christian community whose practices and skills he had been working so hard to develop continued to exist, Bonhoeffer might well have discovered patterns of life in Christian community that would not have required his 'act of repentance'. Thus we think James Wm. McClendon is right in suggesting that the tragedy of Bonhoeffer's life and death is only a part of the larger tragedy of the Christian community in Germany.[81]

Bonhoeffer represents a powerful performance of Scripture, even in the midst of his tragic death. Whatever one's assessment of Bonhoeffer's willingness to take up the sword in the attempt to assasinate Hitler, it is important to recognize that Bonhoeffer did not seek easy ways out or simply abandon his concern with Scripture. He continued to struggle to discern the word of the Lord in a complex and extraordinary time. But Bonhoeffer's efforts were undermined by the eclipse of Christian community in Germany. He was unable to turn to brothers and sisters in Christ to help him discern what ought to be done.

It can justly be said of Bonhoeffer that he 'paid for the word of God with his life and taught it with his death'. We ought also to remember his conviction that even in the midst of the world where God is to be found, we need to develop and maintain the communal practices of something like a 'discipline of the secret' if we are to become people of practical wisdom in our readings of Scripture and of the world. In short, Bonhoeffer's life and death serve as a powerful illustration of the importance of reading in communion.

## NOTES

1. Dietrich Bonhoeffer, *Fiction From Prison*, tr. Ursula Hoffman (Philadelphia, PA: Fortress, 1981), p. 61. We are indebted to David McI. Gracie's 'Introduction' to Bonhoeffer's *Meditating on the Word* (Cambridge, MA: Cowley Publications, 1986), for pointing us to this story of Bonhoeffer's and to the epitaph in particular.

2. This is not to say there have been no studies; see, for examples, Martin Kuske, *The Old Testament as the Book of Christ: An Appraisal of Bonhoeffer's Interpretation*, tr. S. T. Kimbrough Jr (Philadelphia, PA: Westminster, 1976); Walter Harrelson, 'Bonhoeffer and the Bible', in *The Place of Bonhoeffer: Problems and Possibilities in His Thought*, ed. Martin Marty (London: Greenwood Press; New York: Association Press, 1962), pp. 115–42. Gracie's 'Introduction' to *Meditating on the Word* also provides some comments on Bonhoeffer's readings of Scripture.

3. For an example of a place where Bonhoeffer's reading of Scripture is particularly problematic, see his 'A Wedding Sermon from a Prison Cell', in *Letters and Papers from Prison*, enlarged edn, tr. R.H. Fuller *et al.*, ed. Eberhard Bethge (London: SCM; New York: Macmillan, 1972), pp. 41–7.

4. For the details of Bonhoeffer's life, we have drawn most heavily on Bethge's monumental biography, *Dietrich Bonhoeffer*, tr. Edwin Robertson, *et al.* (London: Collins, 1970). Another extremely helpful account on which we have drawn is James W. McClendon's insightful chapter on Bonhoeffer in his *Ethics: Systematic Theology Vol. I*

(Nashville, TN: Abingdon, 1986), pp. 187–208.

5. These three transitions are noted by Bethge, who structures his biography into three similar parts. McClendon's chapter is similarly structured.

6. For a discussion of Bonhoeffer's family, see Renate Bethge, 'Bonhoeffer's Family and Its Significance for His Theology', in Larry Rasmussen, *Dietrich Bonhoeffer – His Significance for North Americans* (Minneapolis, MN: Fortress, 1990), pp. 1–30.

7. Bethge, *Dietrich Bonhoeffer*, pp. 56–7.

8. ibid., p. 113.

9. ibid., p. 113.

10. ibid., p. 86.

11. Bonhoeffer, *Gesammelte Schriften I*, p. 424, cited in Bethge, *Dietrich Bonhoeffer*, p. 113.

12. Bonhoeffer, cited in Bethge, *Dietrich Bonhoeffer*, pp. 154–5.

13. Bonhoeffer, *No Rusty Swords*, tr. C. H. Robertson, *et al.* (London: Collins, 1970), p. 181.

14. Indeed, drawing on lectures and Bible studies Bonhoeffer conducted during 1932, Bethge makes the important point that the concerns of *The Cost of Discipleship* and *Life Together* are not merely responses to the rise of Hitler in 1933. Those concerns precede 1933, and are more directly related to the changes in Bonhoeffer's own understanding of the Bible. See Bethge, *Dietrich Bonhoeffer*, pp. 158–9.

15. Bonhoeffer, *Creation and Fall*, tr. John C. Fletcher (London: SCM, 1959), p. 12.

16. ibid., p. 11.

17. Bethge, *Dietrich Bonhoeffer*, p. 163.

18. The story of Gideon is found in Judges 6–8.

19. Bonhoeffer, cited in Bethge, *Dietrich Bonhoeffer*, p. 228.

20. Bonhoeffer, cited in Bethge, *Dietrich Bonhoeffer*, p. 252.

21. Bonhoeffer, cited in Bethge, *Dietrich Bonhoeffer*, p. 259.

22. See Bethge, *Dietrich Bonhoeffer*, pp. 259 and 273–4.

23. Bonhoeffer in a letter to his grandmother, cited in Bethge, *Dietrich Bonhoeffer*, p. 330.

24. The Confessing Church comprised Christians united in their opposition both to Hitler and to the established Church's support of the Nazis. Their principles are laid out in the Barmen Declaration of 1934.

25. Bonhoeffer, cited in Bethge, *Dietrich Bonhoeffer*, p. 380.

26. Recall our earlier discussion of this 'turning' in Chapter 3.

27. Bonhoeffer, *The Way to Freedom*, tr. Edwin H. Robertson and John Bowden, ed. Edwin H. Robertson (London: Fontana; New York: Harper & Row, 1966), p. 31.

28. Bonhoeffer, cited in Bethge, *Dietrich Bonhoeffer*, p. 383.

29. After the seminary at Finkenwalde was dissolved by the Nazis in 1937, Bonhoeffer published in 1939 an account of the Christian community the seminarians were seeking to embody. See Bonhoeffer, *Life Together*, tr. John W. Doberstein (London: SCM;

New York: Harper & Row, 1954).
30. It is a mistake to see Bonhoeffer's life in terms of a 'churchly' phase in 1932–9 followed by a 'political' phase from 1939 until his death. Bonhoeffer was concerned with political and 'worldly' issues prior to 1939, and he continued his concern with the Church and community after 1939.
31. Bonhoeffer, found in *Dietrich Bonhoeffer: Witness to Jesus Christ*, ed. John de Gruchy (London: Collins, 1987), p. 188. The full English text of Bonhoeffer's lecture is found in *No Rusty Swords*, pp. 302–20.
32. Bonhoeffer, 'The Presentation of New Testament Texts', cited in *Dietrich Bonhoeffer: Witness to Jesus Christ*, ed. de Gruchy, p. 190.
33. ibid., p. 191.
34. See Kuske, *The Old Testament as the Book of Christ*, pp. 41–85, for an excellent evaluation of the exegesis of the three lectures. More generally, we are indebted to Kuske's excellent study for much of our understanding of Bonhoeffer's readings of the Old Testament.
35. ibid., p. 44.
36. See, for example, the German scholar Friedrich Baumgärtel's attack in 1936, *Die Kirche ist Eine – die alttestamentlich – jüdische und die Kirche Jesu Christi? Eine Verwahrung gegen die Preisgabe des Alten Testaments*, and, more recently, the American scholar Walter Harrelson's criticisms in 'Bonhoeffer and the Bible'.
37. See Kuske's discussion of Baumgärtel's objections on this point, in *The Old Testament as the Book of Christ*, p. 83.
38. Ironically, the way the apostle Paul read (what we call) the Old Testament is much closer to Bonhoeffer's way of reading than it is to Bonhoeffer's critics. As Richard Hays has shown in *Echoes of Scripture in the Letters of Paul*, (New Haven, CT: Yale University Press, 1989), Paul exercised an interpretive freedom with Scripture (our Old Testament) in the light of God's revelation in Jesus Christ. Hays argues that Paul read Scripture in terms of election and promise, as a word for and about the community of faith, in the service of proclamation, and as participants in the eschatological drama of redemption (see pp. 183–6).
39. See, for example, Robert P. Ericksen's discussion of Gerhard Kittel's attitude towards the Old Testament in *Theologians Under Hitler* (New Haven, CT: Yale University Press, 1985), pp. 28–78.
40. Here it is important to note that Baumgärtel, though he claimed that his criticisms of Bonhoeffer's reading of Ezra and Nehemiah were neutral in terms of the political issues regnant in Germany, continued to presume that the Jews were responsible for the crucifixion of Jesus. See the discussion in William Jay Peck, 'The Role of the "Enemy" in Bonhoeffer's Life and Thought', in *A Bonhoeffer Legacy*, ed. A. J. Klaasen (Grand Rapids, MI: Wm. B. Eerdmans, 1981), pp. 352–3.
41. Bonhoeffer, *Gesammelte Schriften IV*, p. 320, cited in Kuske, *The Old Testament as the Book of Christ*, p. 49.

42. Bonhoeffer, cited in *Meditating on the Word*, ed. Gracie, p 40.
43. Bonhoeffer, *The Cost of Discipleship*, tr. R. H. Fuller (London: SCM, 1959), pp. 54 and 55.
44. ibid., p. 313.
45. ibid., p. 314.
46. ibid., pp. 158 and 159.
47. ibid., p. 161.
48. Bonhoeffer, cited in Bethge, *Dietrich Bonhoeffer*, p. 512.
49. Indeed, later in his work on *Ethics*, Bonhoeffer would write: 'An expulsion of the Jews from the west must necessarily bring with it the expulsion of Christ. For Jesus Christ was a Jew' (*Ethics*, tr. [from the 6th German edn] Neville H. Smith, and ed. Eberhard Bethge [London: SCM; New York: Macmillan, 1965], p. 90).
50. Bonhoeffer, cited in Bethge, *Dietrich Bonhoeffer*, p. 541. Added emphasis is Bonhoeffer's. See also the discussion in McClendon, *Ethics*, pp. 203–4.
51. Bonhoeffer, cited in Bethge, *Dietrich Bonhoeffer*, p. 559.
52. When Bonhoeffer was deciding whether to return to Germany, the *Losung* text (the *Losungen* was a collection of brief texts designed for meditation through the year) for 26 June was from 2 Timothy 4.21, 'Do your best to come before winter.' Bonhoeffer's comment, cited in Bethge, *Dietrich Bonhoeffer*, p. 560, is revealing: 'That follows me around all day. It is as if we were soldiers home on leave, and going back into action regardless of what they were to expect. We cannot be released from it…"Do your best to come before winter" – it is not a misuse of Scripture if I apply it to myself. May God give me grace to do it.'
53. The fragments have been compiled and edited by Eberhard Bethge and published as Dietrich Bonhoeffer, *Ethics*.
54. Bonhoeffer, *The Cost of Discipleship*, p. 127.
55. Indeed, he repeats the claim almost directly, and then develops it more fully. See *Ethics*, p. 60.
56. Bonhoeffer, *Ethics*, p. 59.
57. In the context of his argument that Bonhoeffer was concerned with politics throughout his life, William Jay Peck contends that these two sayings apply throughout Bonhoeffer's life. Peck's main point is true, but his particular claim that Bonhoeffer had understood the importance of 'he that is not against us is for us' prior to the resistance seems tenuous at best. See Peck, 'The Role of the "Enemy" in Bonhoeffer's Life and Thought', p. 358, n. 15.
58. See Bonhoeffer, *Ethics*, p. 206.
59. Larry Rasmussen, *Dietrich Bonhoeffer: Reality and Resistance* (Nashville, TN: Abingdon, 1972), p. 22.
60. Bonhoeffer, *Ethics*, p. 197. An excellent discussion of Bonhoeffer's rejection of 'two spheres' thinking is found in Ernst Feil, *The Theology of Dietrich Bonhoeffer*, tr. Martin Rumscheidt (Philadelphia, PA: Fortress, 1985), pp. 146ff.
61. Bonhoeffer, *Ethics*, p. 198.

62. See Bonhoeffer, *Letters and Papers from Prison*, p. 279.
63. Bonhoeffer, *Ethics*, p. 85.
64. See Rasmussen, *Dietrich Bonhoeffer*, pp. 42ff., for an excellent discussion of these issues, to which we are greatly indebted.
65. Bonhoeffer, *Ethics*, pp. 130–1. Bonhoeffer's conviction that Christology must embrace incarnation, crucifixion and resurrection did not emerge only in his later work; even in his student notes in the 1920s Bonhoeffer stressed the importance of the whole scope of Christ's person and work.
66. Rasmussen, *Dietrich Bonhoeffer*, p. 43. Bonhoeffer's construal would have been enriched had he placed these marks of Christ's life in relation to the Triune God.
67. Bonhoeffer, *Letters and Papers from Prison*, p. 303. Rasmussen's comment on this passage is instructive: 'The polyphony of life is the shape of grace and the means to maturity' (*Dietrich Bonhoeffer*, p. 43, n. 70).
68. Bonhoeffer, *Letters and Papers from Prison*, pp. 369–70.
69. There are only two letters where Bonhoeffer actually refers to the arcane discipline, though its constructive significance in Bonhoeffer's thought looms much larger. See *Letters and Papers from Prison*, pp. 281 and 286. For a recent discussion of its importance in Bonhoeffer's thought, see Larry Rasmussen, 'Worship in a World Come of Age' in *Dietrich Bonhoeffer – His Significance for North Americans*, pp. 57–71.
70. Bonhoeffer, *Letters and Papers from Prison*, pp. 282 and 382.
71. Even so, Kenneth Surin has drawn on the arguments of Max Weber and Theodor Adorno in arguing that Bonhoeffer's own account of the 'discipline of the secret' is, while provocative, unable to withstand the pressures of the contemporary world which Bonhoeffer otherwise attends to so carefully. To oversimplify an important and complex argument, Surin's point is that (in our terms) Bonhoeffer's 'readings of the world' are inadequate. We are not completely convinced by Surin's analysis, but his argument is important. See Kenneth Surin, '*Contemptus Mundi* and the disenchantment of the world', in his *The Turnings of Darkness and Light* (Cambridge: Cambridge University Press, 1989), pp. 180–200.
72. Bonhoeffer, cited in Rasmussen, *Dietrich Bonhoeffer*, p. 25.
73. Once again, a fully trinitarian hermeneutic would have enriched and made more complete the Christological claims Bonhoeffer makes. In his paper for Seeberg, Bonhoeffer had argued for the importance of a pneumatological exegesis, but that emphasis on the Spirit does not seem to continue in his developing readings of the Old Testament or, for that matter, in his theological reflections more generally.
74. Bonhoeffer, *Letters and Papers from Prison*, p. 315.
75. ibid., p. 282.
76. See Kuske, *The Old Testament as the Book of Christ*, pp. 150ff.
77. Bonhoeffer, *Letters and Papers from Prison*, p. 157.
78. Cited in Bethge, *Dietrich Bonhoeffer*, p. 530.

79. An excellent discussion of Bonhoeffer's understanding of guilt, particularly in relation to Church, nation and class, is found in Rasmussen, *Dietrich Bonhoeffer*, pp. 55–63. The reference to Bonhoeffer's own understanding of his participation in the resistance as an act of repentance is recorded by Bishop George Bell, 'The Background of the Hitler Plot', *Contemporary Review* (October 1945), p. 206.

80. The wording comes from Bonhoeffer's work on a catechism in 1936, cited in Bethge, *Dietrich Bonhoeffer*, p. 144. There is no reason to believe that he changed his view later, as even here he is speaking of the Christian taking up a sword in a just cause. It is unclear why, if the participation is justified, Bonhoeffer also thought that a person would need forgiveness. Bonhoeffer's attitude towards war in general, and the question of whether or not he was a pacifist in particular, is a controversial matter. Rasmussen's discussion in *Dietrich Bonhoeffer: Reality and Resistance* provides the best overview of the issues both in Bonhoeffer's thought and in his life.

81. McClendon, *Ethics* pp. 206–7. We are not as convinced as McClendon that the willingness to assassinate Hitler was 'inconsistent with Bonhoeffer's long formed Christian convictions', at least on Bonhoeffer's own understanding. Bonhoeffer was not so clearly a pacifist as such a comment would suggest. Even so, we share McClendon's general assessment of the tragedy of Bonhoeffer's life and death.

# INDEX OF NAMES